THE
TWO FACES
OF
JESUS

Christmas 1993.

Dear Peter & Janet,

    I hope this is helpful
in your reading preparation
for the coming year's adventure.

    with much love in Christ,

       Priscilla.

THE TWO FACES OF JESUS

PAUL BARNETT

Hodder & Stoughton

SYDNEY AUCKLAND LONDON TORONTO

ACKNOWLEDGEMENTS The author wishes to thank the following publishers for permission to quote from works for which they hold copyright: J.C.B. Mohr (Paul Siebeck), *The Son of Man as the Son of God*, by S. Kim; William Collins, *Jesus the Jew* by G. Vermes; SCM Press, *Jesus and Judaism* by E.P. Sanders.

The Bible text in this publication is from the Revised Standard Version of the Bible unless otherwise indicated.

First published in 1990 by
Hodder & Stoughton (Australia) Pty Limited
10–16 South Street, Rydalmere, NSW 2116
© Paul W. Barnett, 1990

National Library of Australia Cataloguing-in-Publication entry
Barnett, Paul (Paul William)
    The Two Faces of Jesus
    Includes maps, tables.
    ISBN 0 340 53602 0.
    1. Jesus Christ - Historicity. 2. Jesus Christ
    - Biography - Sources. I. Title.
232.908

Typeset in Australia by G.T. Setters Pty Limited
Printed by The Book Printer, Maryborough, Victoria.

CONTENTS

To
my children
Sarah, Anne, Peter and David

1 A New Quest for Jesus

A "New Quest" for the historical Jesus has arisen which sets Jesus firmly within a Jewish context. However, many of its scholars view Jesus in ways Christians will find disturbing.

I write this book from the conviction that, in the next few years, Christianity will face a challenge over the identity of its founder, Jesus Christ. Unnoticed by the great majority of Christians some very interesting developments in Jesus research have occurred during the past twenty years. Soon the greater knowledge about Jesus will be out in the open and its impact more widely felt.

This is a serious matter since Christianity is based on a particular attitude to the identity of Jesus. If Christians were to lose confidence that Jesus is the Son of God, the foundation of the faith would be eroded and the edifice of Christianity would crumble and fall within a few generations.

What is this challenge over the identity of Jesus?

During the past two decades there has quietly arisen a "New Quest" for the historical Jesus—that is the quest for authentic information about the human Jesus as he really was, as a historical person.

The "Old Quest", which arose in the romantic era of the nineteenth century and which depicted Jesus in heroic terms was effectively overturned by Albert Schweitzer's famous work, *The Quest of the Historical Jesus*, originally published in 1906. From that time until the last two decades scholars felt that little could be said about the historical Jesus. In

1934 Rudolph Bultmann reflecting sceptically on the Old Quest wrote, "We can now know almost nothing concerning the life and personality of Jesus..." (*Jesus and the Word*, p.14.)

The New Quest scholars, however, believe that we can now know a great deal about Jesus of Nazareth. In 1985 E.P. Sanders, demonstrating the confidence of the New Quest, wrote:

> We can know pretty well what Jesus was out to accomplish...we can know a lot about what he said, and that those two things make sense in the world of first-century Judaism. (*Jesus and Judaism*, p.2.)

The pendulum has swung to the other extreme.

Sanders' last comment is critical. The Jesus, whom we can now "know a lot about" is seen to "make sense in the world of first-century Judaism". He is Jesus with a Jewish face, a "son of the synagogue". The New Quest for the historical Jesus is focused on his Jewishness.

Why is there now this emphasis on the Jewishness of Jesus?

Four developments since the end of World War II should be noted.

One has been the consolidation of the modern state of Israel since the six-day war in 1967 when virtually all of Palestine, including Jerusalem, came under Israeli occupation. This has made possible extensive archaeological investigation of Jerusalem and other sites visited by Jesus, so that much more is now known about his life and times (see, for example, J.H. Charlesworth, *Jesus Within Judaism*, pp.103–127). Significantly, Bultmann never visited Israel.

Moreover, many scholars repulsed by the antisemitism of the Nazis and indeed by the writings of numbers of Christian scholars of earlier generations, are now glad to acknowledge that Jesus truly was a Jew. Today Jewish and Gentile scholars engage in Jesus research without antipathy.

Further, the methods of sociology have begun to be applied to various religious and political groups which are described in the writings of the New Testament and Josephus, a Jewish historian who wrote in the last quarter of the first century. These movements and their leaders have now been subjected to careful social analysis. Scholars have asked: "To which social group within first century Judaism does Jesus belong? Is he a Pharisee, a Sadducee, a Prophet, a Zealot, a member of the Qumran community?"

Finally, in recent times, much study has been devoted to the literature of Judaism at that time. The discovery of the Dead Sea Scrolls in 1947 sparked off extensive research into the sect which lived on the north-western side of the Dead Sea, a sect which was active at the time of Jesus. But there has also been a remarkable interest shown in other Jewish literature of that general period—like the historical writings of Josephus and the Mishnah which appeared about AD 200, but which quoted from rabbis who were teaching at the time of Jesus.

As a result of these labours by both Jewish and Gentile scholars much more is known of the world of Jesus' times than was available when Rudolph Bultmann was writing. Whatever he was, the New Quest scholars insist, Jesus of Nazareth was a Jew.

From many points of view this emphasis is thoroughly welcome. It stresses the genuine humanity of Jesus as a true figure of history. It is now clear that Jesus had an identifiable cultural and historical context, just as we have. He spoke Aramaic; a number of his statements in his mother tongue survive within the Gospels, notably his cry from the cross. He taught and debated in the style of a Jewish rabbi, and indeed was regularly addressed as "rabbi". Jesus appealed to the Jewish scriptures, upheld orthodox Jewish beliefs about the resurrection and the final judgement of God, attended the Passover and other Jewish feasts, and believed in Yahweh the God of Israel who had been revealed in the Old Testament. Numbers of Jesus' sayings and parables are paralleled with other Jewish writings of his period. In Paul's words Jesus was "born under the law" (Galatians 4:4). Jesus was a Jew.

However, there are problems. Not all the New Quest scholars reach conclusions about Jesus with which orthodox Christians will feel comfortable. Indeed the New Quest scholars may be broadly divided into two groups. On one hand, J.H. Charlesworth, for example, whose *Jesus within*

Judaism was published in 1988, clearly affirms Jesus to be the Son of God in a sense traditionally understood by Christians.

On the other hand—and herein lies the challenge to which I am referring—many New Quest scholars explicitly or implicitly deny that Jesus was the Son of God in the sense understood by the Christian creeds. Jesus is culturally imprisoned within the walls of first century Judaism. This Jesus is no longer "Lord of *all*"—Lord of both Jews *and* Gentiles—as the New Testament proclaims him to be.

It is not that the negative New Quest scholars—if for convenience I may so describe them—are agreed about the identity of this Jewish Jesus. While doubting that Jesus is the Son of God and the second person of the Trinity there is no consensus as to who Jesus was or what his role and mission was.

In 1967 Samuel Brandon located Jesus within the political stream of Judaism, among those nationalist Jews who sought deliverance from their Roman overlords. Brandon saw Jesus as a "zealot" or as an active sympathizer of the zealot cause of national liberation. (Brandon is probably too early, and his nationalistic emphases too extreme, to be grouped with the New Quest scholars.)

Indeed, for most New Quest scholars Jesus is not a man of violence but of peace. For Max Wilcox, who wrote in 1982, Jesus is above all a devout rabbi, a non-violent man:

> He. . . resembles. . . a hasid, a pious man whose emphasis in matters of *halakhah* (= behaviour) is more stringent in duty to fellow man and less so in questions of 'purity' and table fellowship than is the case with acceptable Pharisaic norms (*ANRW*, p.185).

As such, as many Jewish and Gentile scholars agree, Jesus was and remains an admirable man, whose teachings and personal example continue to inspire all those with whom he has contact. Geza Vermes concludes his epoch-making work *Jesus the Jew*, written in 1973, with these words:

> The earliest gospel tradition, considered against the background of first century Galilean charismatic religion, leads. . . to a Jesus [who is] Jesus the just man, the *zaddik*, Jesus the helper and healer, Jesus the teacher and leader,

venerated by his intimates and less committed admirers
alike as prophet, lord and son of God.

For Vermes, "lord" and "son of God" are not titles of deity,
as in the creeds of the Church, but titles of honour
appropriate for rabbis of the period. Since then Vermes' views
have often been re-stated, with refinements. (See Swidler,
pp.95–108.)

In Sanders' *Jesus and Judaism* (1984) Jesus is presented
as an "eschatological charismatic" prophet who proclaimed
a coming other-worldly kingdom of a restored Judaism.
Sanders thinks Jesus may have regarded himself as being
some type of "viceroy" in that kingdom.

R.A. Horsley and J.S. Hanson (1985) suggest that Jesus
should be thought of as one of the popular prophets of the
period—like John the Baptist or Theudas. "The [two types]
of popular prophets clearly provide the most potentially
fruitful comparative materials for exploration of aspects of
Jesus' career" (*Bandits, Prophets and Messiahs*, p.257.)

While these scholars express a range of opinions it is
possible to narrow their definitions of Jesus to two roles in
particular—those of rabbi or prophet.

It is not that these New Quest scholars necessarily portray
Jesus in a way that offends Christians. For the Jews of his
day Jesus would have been regarded as some kind of a rabbi
or a prophet. Later Jewish literature would describe Jesus
as a false teacher and charlatan, a man of uncertain
parentage. For the scholars to whom I am referring, however,
Jesus is one of the recognised teachers within Judaism and
a sound moral example. But therein may lie the danger of
our understanding of Jesus; in their reconstructions Jesus
is not the Son of God, not the Lord. Indeed, given the
essential monotheism of Judaism no true Jew could have
made such blasphemous claims. Jesus the true Jew, whose
most fundamental belief was that Yahweh his God was One
(Deuteronomy 6:4), that is indivisible, could not possibly have
regarded himself as the Son of God in the sense later
understood by Christians.

These New Quest scholars tend to deny two further
fundamental teachings of traditional Christianity.

First, belief in the second advent of the Son of Man, they

say, rests on a misunderstanding of Jewish idiom. In referring to the coming of the Son of Man Jesus was really prophesying the destruction of the temple.

Second, the call by Jesus for a specific mission to the Gentiles. This, they claim, also rests on a misunderstanding. No Jew committed to Yahweh's cause for his people could have included the Gentiles in Yahweh's saving plans.

It is argued that these doctrines of Christianity, as it was to develop within the New Testament and later, obscure our understanding about Jesus' real character. According to these scholars Jesus should be seen as a remarkable, though not unique, Jew of the second temple period, whose teachings have ethical but not faith-commitment significance.

If we ask how it was that, within a few years, Jesus became the object not merely of imitation but of worship these authors are compelled to say that the early church re-defined Jesus, that a distortion of the historical Jesus has occurred.

That a considerable body of front rank scholars now hold to the negative New Quest view of Jesus is serious for Christian faith and devotion. Inevitably these views have not remained confined within the halls of learning but have begun to filter through the popular media to the general public. Herein lies the challenge for the future of traditional Christianity.

In a major television documentary *Jesus the Evidence*, which appeared in the 1980s, the negative New Quest view was quite prominent. This proved to be highly controversial and deeply unsettling to many Christians.

Major surveys of expert opinion about Jesus' identity have appeared in the popular press during the 1980s. One by Cullen Murphy appeared in Atlanta, and was reproduced in many countries. The other was the cover story for *Time* Magazine. Both asked the question: "Who was Jesus?" Both quoted numerous scholarly opinions, including those of the New Quest, which many people found disturbing.

The popular perception could soon be that, because many scholars claim that the church has misrepresented Jesus, Christian belief is discredited.

But, you may ask, am I not overstating the situation? Surely during the last two centuries many scholars in the liberal tradition have presented a humanistic view of Jesus. What is new about this crisis?

The new factor is that the New Quest scholarship, including those who take a negative view of Jesus' deity, is very accomplished in an area which is inaccessible to most, namely that of first century Jewish studies. Even among New Testament scholars few are expert in first century Jewish history and literature, to say nothing of the average Christian. The problem is that the exponents of the New Quest, including those who take a negative view of Jesus' deity, are highly respected scholars.

The implications for Christians today are serious. If the confession that Jesus is the Son of God and the Lord—the object of divine worship as affirmed in the Creeds of the Church—rests on misunderstanding and distortion, then the chief focus of the faith is clouded. In this case Jesus may be of interest to a handful of scholars of Jewish antiquity as just one in the passing parade of intriguing, but ultimately irrelevant rabbis and prophets of the first century.

Before proceeding it is appropriate that I lay my own cards on the table. I write as a Christian believer. I regard Jesus as the Son of God, as the creeds state. I arrived at that conclusion quite a few years ago, though I have re-examined it recently in the light of other opinions such as those set out above. This little book has arisen out of these further investigations. The area of study in which I have been engaged for some time has been revolutionary groups like the zealots and various apocalyptic prophets from the first century.

The approach to the subject taken here is historical; it is not in terms of systematic or dogmatic theology. If the questioning of Jesus' identity is being made on the basis of historical evidence then the response needs to be made on the same basis.

I will not merely expand on what the creeds say about Jesus. Rather, I will present a profile of Jesus, his mission and identity, based on historical analysis of the available evidence.

This is not a technical book, however, intended only for specialists but for the reader who is prepared to follow a line of argument and then decide, one way or the other, who Jesus was. (Some books and articles for further reference are to be found at the end of each chapter.)

Nor is this book part of a running debate with those scholars from whose opinions of Jesus I respectfully differ. Such a book would be both long and involved. Having set out the salient points made by some spokesmen I will concentrate on establishing that Jesus the Jew is the Son of God and the Lord of all, based on the evidence of the New Testament which is set within the context of first century Judaism.

In what follows I will offer an explanation for this polarization between those who affirm and those who deny Jesus' deity. These diverging perceptions of Jesus, however, have not merely arisen in modern times; they go back to the time of Jesus himself.

Further reading:

M.J. Borg, *Conflict, Holiness and Politics in the Teachings of Jesus,* (New York and Toronto, Edwin Mellen Press., 1984)

S.G.F. Brandon, *Jesus and the Zealots*, (Manchester, University Press, 1967)

C. Brown, *Jesus in European Protestant Thought 1778–1860,* (Grand Rapids, Baker, 1988)

R. Bultmann, *Jesus and the Word*, (London, Fontana, 1958)

G.B. Caird, "Jesus and Israel: The Starting Point for New Testament Christology" in *Christological Perspectives,* ed. R. Berkey and S. Edwards, pp.58–68.

J.H. Charlesworth, *Jesus Within Judaism,* (London, SPCK, 1988)

J.D.G. Dunn, *The Evidence for Jesus*, (London, SCM, 1985)

M. Hengel, *The Charismatic Leader and His Followers*, (Edinburgh, Clark, 1981)

J. Jeremias, *New Testament Theology*, (London, SCM, 1971)

J. Riches, *Jesus and the Transformation of Judaism,* (London, Darton, Longman and Todd, 1980)

E.P. Sanders, *Jesus and Judaism*, (London, SCM Press, 1984)

A. Schweitzer, *The Quest of the Historical Jesus*, (London, SCM, 1981)

L. Swidler, "Contemporary Implications of the Jewish-Christian Dialogue on Jesus Christ", *Dialogue and Alliance* 2/3 (1988) pp.95–108

G. Vermes, *Jesus the Jew*, (London, Collins, 1973)

M. Wilcox, "Jesus in the Light of His Jewish Environment", *Aufstieg und Niedergang der römischen Welt*, ii, (1982), pp.131–195

N.T. Wright, "Jesus, Israel and the Cross", the Society of Biblical Literature, *Seminar Papers*, 1985, pp.70–95

2 THE TWO FACES OF JESUS

*Jesus has two sides, or faces—the public and the "filial"
faces. Those who see only the public face will always
be uncertain of his true identity.*

There is a problem in responding to the (negative) New Quest
views of Jesus. It is that these scholars have genuine historical
insights into Jesus. Much of what they observe about Jesus
as rabbi or prophet is helpful for our understanding. The
difficulty is not what they affirm, but what they deny,
implicitly or explicitly—that Jesus is the Son of God in the
sense traditionally understood by Christians.

My aim in writing this book is to do justice to what these
scholars helpfully contribute to our understanding about
Jesus, whilst re-affirming what they deny about him. I will
also attempt to explain how it is that the diverging views of
Jesus' identity arise. To that end I will use throughout this
book a controlling analogy—the human face.

In this regard, I make two explanatory comments.

First, it is by my face that I am recognised and identified.
It is a photo of my face, not my limbs or organs, which
appears within my passport.

Second, the human face can be thought of as having two
sides, as being two faces. The people of the Old Testament
thought of a person as having two faces; they used the plural
word *pan'im*—faces—even for one person. Did he not have
two eyes, two ears, two nostrils, two faces?

Using this analogy I will argue that Jesus showed two
different faces—or sides of himself—to the people of that
time. The Jewish people of the time saw only one face, the
face of a synagogue teacher and prophet. I shall refer to this

as the *public* face of Jesus. As historians, standing in the shoes of Jesus' contemporaries, the New Quest scholars with whom I differ also see that face, the face of Jesus as a rabbi or a prophet.

But there was another face—the *filial* face of Jesus, the face of the Son of God. (*Filius* is Latin for "son".) Jesus showed that face to the Twelve. Along with other Jews the Twelve saw the public face but they were also privileged to see another face of Jesus which people generally did not see, for Jesus showed his filial face only to the Twelve.

One's view of Jesus will depend on which face one has seen. Those who have seen the filial face of Jesus will regard him as the Son of God, a unique person who enjoyed a singular relationship with God. He is the Son of God who is Lord of all.

But those who have seen only the public face of Jesus will be uncertain about his identity. Who is he? If he is viewed in minimal terms as a prophet or a rabbi, how are we to explain his miracles and the survival and growth of early Christianity? Perhaps he is to be interpreted in dark and sinister terms as mad or evil? In his own day those not privileged to see his filial face passed similarly conflicting verdicts about him. While the people at large thought he was a prophet (Mark 8:28) or even the Messiah (John 10:24), his own family thought he was mad (Mark 3:21; cf. John 10:20) and the religious teachers regarded him as demon-possessed (Mark 3:22; John 10:20), a false teacher and a blasphemer (John 9:16; 10:33; Mark 2:6). For those who still see only his public face Jesus remains to this day an enigma, a riddle. New theories will continue to appear, new books be written, as successive generations struggle to understand this man.

I should explain that the analogy of the two faces does not refer to the two natures—the human and the divine—in Jesus. Christians of the fourth and fifth centuries tried to comprehend the paradox of one person having two different natures. This is not the subject of this book. Rather, our analogy of the two faces refers to the two perceptions of Jesus which arose at the time and which are still current today in the debate which has been stimulated by the New Quest scholars.

3 Jesus in History

New Quest scholars have reminded us of the need to see Jesus as truly human, as a genuine figure of history—Jewish history—in the first half of the first century.

Part of Jesus' mystique is that relatively little is known about him prior to the four years in which he was a public figure. This is dramatised in Mark's presentation where Jesus simply appears on the scene, ready to commence his ministry, without any prior information being given about him. The letter to the Hebrews refers to Jesus in terms of Melchizedek, a mysterious king from patriarchal days, who was "without father or mother or genealogy" who had "neither beginning of days nor end of life" (7:3), and who simply appeared unannounced to Abraham.

Possibly this is the reason Jesus has been seen as detached from history, to have been somehow de-judaized. Jesus' public face has been all but denied by Christians. In their favour it must be said that the New Quest scholars have attempted to correct this almost mythical view of Jesus which has been held by many within the church. It is very important to know as much as possible about the public face of Jesus.

While we should not speculate about what Jesus may have done during the so-called "hidden years" between his birth and public ministry we are able to recover quite a lot about the life and times in which he was born, nurtured and matured.

Through the work of archaeologists and scholars of

Judaism the historical and cultural context Jesus of Nazareth is now better understood. We have a reasonable knowledge of the pressures and influences to which he was subject. The greater knowledge of Jesus' era compensates to a degree for our lack of knowledge about him before he emerges as a public figure.

JESUS' BIRTH

Matthew and Luke are our only sources of direct information about Jesus' birth. Although written independently of each other, Matthew and Luke agree about the following details:

1 Joseph, the boy's legal father, belonged to the tribe of Judah and was a descendant of King David, from whose line the Messiah was to come.

2 Mary the mother of Jesus had only been betrothed to Joseph when she became pregnant; Joseph was not the boy's biological father.

3 Joseph married Mary before the child's birth, which occurred in Bethlehem, King David's home town, located six miles south of Jerusalem.

4 Jesus was brought up in Nazareth, an out of the way village in the ranges of lower Galilee, located midway between the Mediterrannean coast and the Sea of Galilee.

JESUS' BOYHOOD

Information from the Gospels about Jesus' boyhood is very limited. However this data may be augmented by what is known of the educational practices of the time.

1 Other children were born to Joseph and Mary—sisters whose names are not given, and four brothers: James, Joseph, Judas and Simon (Mark 6:3). Jesus was the eldest of a family of at least seven children.

2 Also residing in Nazareth were members of Jesus' extended family—uncles, aunts, cousins and possibly grandparents (Mark 6:4; Luke 2:44).

3 The primary intellectual influences on Jesus would have been his father and the synagogue, which educated boys during the week in reading the Torah and which taught the scriptures to those who gathered there on the Sabbath. Philo, an Alexandrian Jew of the middle of the first century, wrote:

> Before any instruction in the holy laws and unwritten customs [children] are taught... from their swaddling clothes by parents, teachers and educators to believe in God, the One Father and Creator of the world. (*Embassy to Gaius* 115)

4 Joseph was a *tekton*, a tradesman who worked in hard materials like timber, metal and stone, and would have been involved in a range of building and repair work in and around Nazareth.

5 As was customary Jesus took up his father's trade (Mark 6:3). A good son-to-father, pupil-teacher relationship between Jesus and Joseph is implied by Jesus' teaching about God as a Father and Teacher. For example,

> The son can do nothing of his own accord but only what he sees the father doing, for the father loves the son, and shows him all that he himself is doing. (John 5:19-20)

6 We know that Jesus was able to read aloud and also to write (Luke 4:16-17; John 8:6), skills which he doubtless learned in the synagogue school which he would have attended from early boyhood.

7 At the age of twelve, when his parents took him for the first time to Jerusalem for Passover, Jesus engaged in technical legal debate with the teachers of the Jewish law (Luke 2:46-47). During his public ministry Jesus revealed formidable ability in formal debate with the scribes, despite not having studied in the rabbinic academies in Jerusalem. Jesus attributed his abilities directly to God (John 7:15). Quite possibly Jesus was the most gifted rabbi of his times. Scribes from Jerusalem had to come to Galilee to debate with him; presumably the local scribes were not equal to the task (Mark 3:22;7:1). Nothing that

survives from the rabbis' teaching of those times
approaches the power of Jesus' teaching.

8 The scriptures were written in Hebrew, which was the
language of the scribes. The people at large conversed in
the various dialects of Aramaic, a Semitic language which
had spread throughout the Middle East in Persian times.
In the previous three centuries, however, the Greek
language had also become widely disseminated throughout
the eastern Mediterranean, including both Galilee and
Judaea. It is probable that Jesus could read and write
Hebrew and Aramaic and that he had some familiarity
with Greek. For example, he often uses the word
"hypocrite" which is a Greek word literally meaning "play
actor", a word for which there is no counterpart in Hebrew
or Aramaic.

9 Jesus' parables show that he was extraordinarily
observant of human affairs and also of the natural and
agricultural environment in which he lived. It is apparent
from the form of Jesus' sayings, and from the dramatic
power of his parables that he was an exceptional teacher.

JESUS' LIFE

There is nothing else we know about Jesus in the years before
he emerged into the full light of public ministry in his thirties.
In the absence of information it is pointless to guess what
might have happened to Jesus in this period. Nonetheless
we are able to sketch the historical period through which
Jesus lived, so as to have some appreciation of the influences
to which he would have been subject at various stages in his
development. Our chief sources of data are the historians
Josephus and Tacitus, the Gospels themselves and
archaeological discoveries.

At the time of Jesus' birth in 7 BC Herod the Great was
approaching the end of his life. To escape the old king's evil
designs on the child's life Joseph and Mary with the infant
Jesus fled to Egypt where they remained for some years.

The death of Herod in 4 BC after a long and repressive
reign was followed by serious instability. The late king's will

was disputed by his sons and other relatives. It was necessary for the family to go to Rome for Augustus to decide who was to succeed Herod. While this was happening uprisings broke out in the major regions of Herod's kingdom. Three self-styled "kings" rose up—Judas in Galilee, Simon in Peraea and Athronges in Judaea. Varus, the Roman general had to bring his legions down from Syria to put down these regional insurrections.

Augustus decided that Herod's kingdom was to be divided into three parts. Archelaus was to rule Judaea and Samaria, about half of the old kingdom; he was given the title "Ethnarch". Antipas was to rule Galilee-Peraea and Philip Gaulanitis; they were each given the lesser title "Tetrarch" (= ruler of a fourth segment).

In c.2 BC, after these troubles had been resolved, Joseph returned from Egypt and settled in Nazareth in Galilee, within the tetrarchy of the teenaged Antipas.

Antipas' older brother Archelaus proved not to be an effective ruler of Judaea, so in AD 6 Augustus removed him. Augustus then took the momentous step of introducing direct Roman rule of Judaea, homeland of God's holy people, where Jerusalem and its massive temple were located. Henceforth the people of Judaea were to be governed by a pagan, a Roman military officer (called a "prefect") whose garrison would be based at Herod's great seaport, Caesarea Maritima.

The day-to-day administration of the new province, however, would fall to the high priest of the temple and his close relatives, who with the aristocratic faction known as the Sadducees now became extremely powerful. One family, whose leading member was Annas, would secure a stranglehold on Judaean politics for the next thirty-five years. His son-in-law Caiaphas became the high priest in AD 18 and it would be during his time that Jesus emerged as a public figure and at whose decision he would be killed as a threat to the national interest (John 11:48).

The introduction of Roman rule in Judaea in AD 6 meant the introduction of a personal tax which was to be paid directly to the Roman emperor. This provoked an uprising

MAP 1:
THE KINGDOM OF HEROD THE GREAT 4 BC

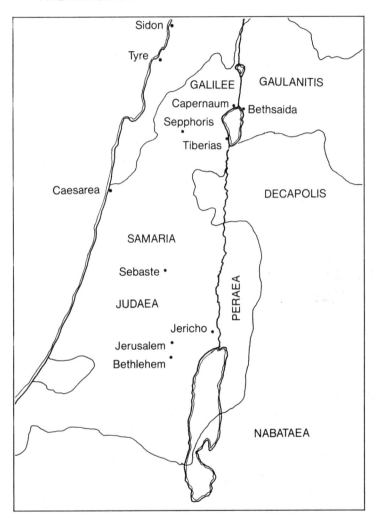

led by Judas the Galilean and a Pharisee name Saddok. These men preached that the tax meant effective slavery to the Romans. They said that God alone was to be Leader and Master and called God's holy people to armed resistance. The Romans crushed the uprising in c. AD 7, that is when Jesus was about fourteen years of age. It is possible that he saw the crosses on which the insurgents were crucified for their defiance of Roman rule, when he came to Jerusalem for the Passover or one of the other major feasts. But revolution now simmered just below the surface of Judaea, ready to erupt at any time.

Whenever Jesus came to Jerusalem for the great feasts he was reminded of the Roman rule of Judaea and of their appointed administrators of the province, the high priests. Passover week in Jerusalem in particular was a highly volatile time. Jews from many quarters converged on the Holy City in tens of thousands and Roman troops were on hand to put down any sudden uprising.

Galilee, where Jesus lived, however, was less explosive, more politically stable—Antipas was the most capable of Herod's sons. Although Herod had named him "king" of his whole realm in an earlier will, Antipas had to be content with the inferior title "tetrarch", ruling a mere quarter of Herod's kingdom, the little-known, landlocked region of Galilee-Peraea. Antipas ruled his region for more than forty years, until he was banished by the mad emperor, Caligula for daring to request his title be upgraded to "king".

Nazareth the town in which Jesus grew up was only four miles from Sepphoris, Antipas' seat of government. When therefore Jesus began his public ministry he treated Antipas with great respect, calling him "that fox" and warning his followers about the "leaven" of his paranoid suspicion (Mark 8:15). Had Antipas not removed John the Baptist for his political preaching to the masses? Jesus' care in not allowing himself to be referred to as "Messiah" was probably due, in part, to his awareness of Antipas' network of spies which would quickly bring such news to the attention of the tetrarch. It is significant that Jesus did not teach near Tiberias, which was built as Antipas' new capital in 20, nor appear in public within Galilee after the Galileans attempted to make him "king" (John 6:14-15).

Galilee was a fertile region which supported two hundred and four sizable towns as well as numerous villages. The area was subdivided into five toparchies or administrative regions. Each town had its leading official who, with the toparchs and military leaders, formed a bureaucracy whose members were dependent on the continuing patronage of Antipas. The land owned by the poor was progressively absorbed into the holdings of the handful of local aristocrats. These also depended on the indulgence of Antipas and formed, with the bureaucrats and the military, the faction known as the "Herodians" (Mark 3:6; 12:13). Many of these dispossessed peasants doubtless formed part of the great crowds which gathered to hear the prophet from Nazareth.

The people whom Jesus would address in the local synagogues and in the open lived in fear of the semi-pagan Antipas and his network of relatives, employees and dependants, under whom they had become progressively impoverished.

In 26, when Jesus was in his early thirties, the emperor Tiberius made a decision which was to have major consequences in the distant province of Judaea. In that year Tiberius retired from public life in Rome to the seclusion of the Island of Capri in the Bay of Naples. In his absence from Rome the sinister Praetorian Prefect L. Aelius Sejanus became de facto emperor. It appears that Sejanus had a strong dislike for the Jewish people and for that reason appointed Pontius Pilate as the new prefect of Judaea.

Even allowing for their obvious bias against him, the Jewish authors Josephus and Philo write of Pilate in damning terms, as a cruel and malicious governor. It appears that Sejanus sent Pilate with the specific mission to de-stabilize Judaea. On his arrival in 26 Pilate instructed his legionaries to bring the Roman standards bearing the highly offensive images of the emperor into the sacred precincts of Jerusalem, something no previous governor had done. He minted coins with pagan religious symbols and raided the sacred treasury of the temple for money to build an aqueduct. Pilate's actions stirred into flames the smouldering embers of Jewish religious nationalism.

In c. 28, when Jesus was in his early thirties, a prophet arose in Peraea—John the Baptist. John summoned the people to confess their sins and to be baptized by him in the River Jordan. John prophesied that the long awaited messenger of God was about to appear and that a new age would dawn with his coming. Antipas was alarmed about the political danger John presented to his tetrarchy so he had him imprisoned and later executed.

Throughout this book the view is taken that Jesus was baptized by John sometime in 29 and crucified during the Passover in 33. This is consistent with Luke 3:2 which gives the commencement of John's prophesying as Tiberius' fifteenth year as Emperor (= i.e. 28 or 29). (It should be noted, however, that most scholars favour AD 30 as the date of the crucifixion. See H.W. Hoehner for arguments in favour of the later date.)

Jesus came from Nazareth to Peraea to be baptized by John. A number of John's immediate circle became followers of Jesus as he prepared to commence his own public ministry. They followed him back to Galilee where he waited to make his annual Passover pilgrimage to Jerusalem (John 2:12).

In AD 30 Jesus, in his mid thirties, began to speak and act in public. While John was still active Jesus went to Jerusalem in the spring for the Passover, where he prophesied the destruction of the temple (John 2:13–21). In Samaria late in the same spring, during his return north, Jesus received news of the imprisonment of John the Baptist. This was the signal for Jesus to emerge fully from the shadow of John and begin his own ministry which he did in the summer of 30, in Galilee. This ministry was conducted chiefly in Galilee for the next two years before the fateful feeding incident where the Galileans attempted to make him king.

After that attempt, Jesus spent the next half-year (spring and summer of 32) in semi-seclusion with his disciples to the west, east and north of Galilee. He spent the autumn and winter of 32 in Judaea before coming finally to Jerusalem for the Passover (in spring 33) at which, as he well knew, death awaited him.

Meanwhile in Judaea, Pilate's anti-semitic actions sparked off the flame of smouldering religious nationalism (which had previously erupted in 6–7 when the direct taxation payable to Rome was introduced). Jesus was caught up in this explosion when he made his final visit to Jerusalem. A man named Barabbas had been held in custody for his involvement in what Mark calls "the insurrection" (15:7), which had obviously occurred in the recent past.

The two men crucified with Jesus at the Passover of 33 were not thieves but political prisoners who had almost certainly been involved in the same "insurrection". Pilate would schedule these crucifixions to occur at Passover time to capitalize on the deterrent effect on the thousands of pilgrims who thronged Jerusalem for the most popular of the Jewish festivals.

It was by a miscarriage of justice that Jesus was crucified and Barabbas was released. Barabbas had killed men during the insurrection; Jesus was guilty of no crime against Roman law. Whatever consciousness Jesus had of being the Messiah, he had made no public claims along those lines. Indeed, he consistently spoke of himself in other ways. He was, in fact, blameless of any crime against Jews or Romans. In reality, Jesus was the victim of a bizarre chain of circumstances which began with Tiberius' withdrawal from public life in Rome and which ended with the crucifixion in Judaea at Passover in 33.

It appears that Pilate did not consider Jesus to be guilty of the treason against Rome with which he was charged by the high priests. Nonetheless, Pilate bowed to the pressure they were now able to exert against him, his protector Sejanus having fallen from power in Rome two years earlier. The high priests, who considered Jesus to be a dangerous influence within Judaea, were able to intimidate the prefect to execute Jesus as "king of the Jews". Because Pilate's position was extremely precarious without Sejanus he acceded to their requests and had Jesus crucified with the insurrectionists under the *titulus* "king of the Jews" (see John 11:47; 19:1–13). This general picture of Jesus, which arises out of the Gospels, broadly corresponds with the only non-biblical accounts we have—those of Josephus and Tacitus.

Josephus' account appears to have been subject to some Christian interpolation. With due allowance for that interpolation Josephus states that:

Jesus...a wise man [i.e. a rabbi]...

> He wrought surprising feats and was a teacher. . .
> He was [said to be] the Messiah. . .
> Pilate. . . hearing him accused by men of the highest
> standing among us. . .
> condemned him to be crucified. . .
>
> > (*Jewish Antiquities* xviii, 63-64)

Tacitus, writing about Nero's assault on Christians after the fire of Rome in AD 64 commented: "Christus. . . the Christian[s']. . . founder had undergone the death penalty. . . by sentence of the procurator Pontius Pilatus. . . in Judaea. . ." (*Annals of Imperial Rome* xv, 44).

Josephus and Tacitus support the Gospels' account that the Roman governor Pontius Pilate executed Jesus in Judaea on the grounds of treason—that he was the Messiah, the King of the Jews. Tacitus is in no doubt that Pilate's decision was correct. Josephus' more neutral version, however, is open to other interpretations. Significantly Josephus portrays Jesus as "a teacher" or rabbi, doubtless reflecting the way many Jews saw him.

The overall impact of the data about Jesus, as we have sketched it, helps us see the public face of Jesus. He was a Galilean rabbi or prophet who attracted considerable interest for a few years but who fell foul of the Jewish authorities in Jerusalem who accused him before the Roman prefect for treasonably claiming to be "king of the Jews". For that crime Jesus was crucified by Roman soldiers outside the city walls of Jerusalem during the Passover of AD 33.

This brief sketch of Jesus in history, recoverable and accurate as it is, however shows only one face of Jesus—a face that continues to mystify us. Important questions remain unanswered. For example, how is it that this man, who is not altogether unlike John the Baptist or other prophets or rabbis of the period, came to launch a great world religion which continues to have millions of adherents?

The problem with this "externalized" or purely historical approach is that it leaves unexamined that other face of Jesus, that face revealed to the Twelve where he disclosed his mission and identity (see chapters seven and eight).

Meanwhile, we must ask whether the public face of Jesus as drawn by some New Quest scholars fits in to his Jewish context as neatly as they suggest.

Further reading:

P.W. Barnett, *Bethlehem to Patmos*, (Sydney, Hodder and Stoughton, 1989)

J.H. Charlesworth, *Jesus within Judaism* (London, SPCK, 1989)

S. Freyne, *Galilee from Alexander the Great to Hadrian 323 BCE-135 CE,* (Wilmington, Glazier, 1980)

H.E. Hoehner, *Herod Antipas*, (Zondervan, Grand Rapids, 1980) *Chronological Aspects of the Life of Christ,* (Grand Rapids, Zondervan, 1977)

J. Klausner, *Jesus of Nazareth*, (London, Collier-Macmillan, 1929)

P.L. Maier, "Sejanus, Pilate and the Date of the Crucifixion", *Church History* 37 (1968), pp.3-13

E.M. Meyers and J.F.Strange, *Archaeology, the Rabbis and Early Christianity,* (London, SCM, 1981)

J.A.T. Robinson, *The Priority of John*, (London, SCM, 1985)

E. Schürer, *The History of the Jewish People in the Age of Jesus Christ,* 1-111 (Rev. ed. Edinburgh, T. and T. Clark, 1973, 1979, 1986)

4 JESUS IN JUDAISM

So closely do some scholars identify Jesus with the context of Judaism that he is regarded by them as quite unremarkable. But in fact Jesus stands out against his context rather than merges with it.

According to E.P. Sanders, one of the most prominent scholars in the New Quest, Jesus himself was not a unique figure:

> I do not doubt that in some ways indicated [Jesus] was unique; in some ways everybody is unique. I do not know, however, that he was unique because he claimed more authority than did Theudas and Judas [near contemporary figures with Jesus] (*Jesus and Judaism* p.240)

> Sociologically and psychologically Jesus and his movement are quite comprehensible. In fact, we cannot say that a single one of the things known about Jesus was unique (p.318).

> We cannot even say that Jesus was an uniquely good and great man (p.320).

I do not share this view. Jesus is in fact very difficult to classify in terms of the various groups which were active at that time. As I have studied these revolutionary and prophetic groups, I have come to the conviction that the differences between Jesus and the leaders of those groups, not the similarities, predominate.

Indeed when one comes to think of Jesus in relation to the groupings of the period one is struck, not by the way he may be seen to "fit" into known groups, but by the way he stands out from them. Several brief examples illustrate the point.

The *Sadducees* were a small and socially élite group, who were in league with the Roman authorities. According to Josephus, who came from the same social class, the Sadducees were "boorish" in their behaviour and unloving even to one another (*Jewish War* ii,166). Unlike the Pharisees, the Sadducees did not believe in angels or the resurrection of the dead (Acts 23:8). The high priests, who were drawn from the Sadducee class, were the chief cause of the opposition to Jesus. They arrested him, twisted the evidence and secured his execution at the hands of the Romans (Mark 14:61-63; 15:1-2). Clearly Jesus did not belong to this group.

Nor did Jesus have much in common with the *Qumran Community*. The sect from Qumran on the Dead Sea did not admit to their membership any one with deformities or disabilities:

No madman, or lunatic, or simpleton, or fool, no blind man, or maimed, or lame, or deaf man and no minor, shall enter the Community, for the Angels of Holiness are with them.... (*Damascus Rule* XV)

Jesus' ministry, however, was focused on the very people in need—on demoniacs, diseased and disabled—whom Qumran rejected. By associating with and healing such needy folk Jesus demonstrated the merciful and inclusive nature of God's Kingdom.

The Qumran Community also required its members to "love all the sons of light...and hate all the sons of darkness" (*Community Rule* 1.9). By contrast, Jesus taught "Love your enemy and pray for those who persecute you" (Matthew 5:44). The community Jesus formed was not to be characterised by love for the insider and hatred for the outsider, but by love for all, including the oppressor (Matthew 5:45-48).

Fundamental to the Qumran Community was its separation from wider Jewish society, especially from the great feasts in the temple. The Qumran Community created and observed its own distinct sacred calendar. In contrast, Jesus attended the feasts in Jerusalem according to the mainstream liturgical calendars of Judaism.

Although Jesus shared the *Pharisees*' views about heaven and hell, the Devil and angels, the resurrection of the dead and the final judgement, there were also many points of difference. The Pharisees were a movement of the Jewish laity who, unlike the Qumran Community, did not physically separate from other Jews. Nonetheless they insisted on a ritual and spiritual separation of the law-observing Jew from the non-observing Jew (Mark 2:16). Thus the Pharisees were preoccupied with sabbath keeping, fasting, tithing, purity from physical contact with the ritually unclean, and separation from lawbreakers and Gentiles (Mark 2:18,24; 3:6; 7:1-3). They took as their authority the oral traditions of the scribes (Mark 7:5).

According to the Gospels, however, Jesus, repeatedly broke the Sabbath and failed to fast. He entered the house of sinners and ate with them. He rejected the practice of purificatory washing (Mark 2:14-28; 7:1-2). Jesus rejected the Pharisees' appeal to the tradition of the scribes and appealed instead directly to the written text of the Old Testament (Mark 7:8).

Although Jesus was sufficiently well educated to teach in the synagogues, he does not appear to have done so for very long. His ministry in the synagogues of Capernaum and the region near the northern lakeside (1:21,39) appears to have terminated once the local and Jerusalem scribes began to controvert his teachings (Mark 2:6,16,24; 3:6,22; but cf. 6:2). Opposition from the scribes forced him out of the synagogues into the open, where he addressed large crowds (2:13; 3:7-12; 4:1; 6:34). Jesus seems to have been *persona non grata* with the Pharisaic authorities, including those who came from Jerusalem (Mark 3:22; 7:1) and therefore not welcome to teach in the synagogues (cf. John 9:22; 12:42).

The various *Zealot*-type nationalist leaders who arose from about AD 6 throughout the period until the destruction of Jerusalem in AD 70—leaders like Judas the Galilean and Simon Bar Gioras—adopted a violent lifestyle in pursuit of

Israel's aspirations. They demanded life and death loyalty to their particular group and hatred of the Gentile enemy. But, as we have noted, Jesus taught the love of the enemy (Matthew 5:44-48), foreshadowed the salvation of the Gentiles (Matthew 8:11) and called on his hearers to learn from him, not as one who was violent (Matthew 11:12) but as one who was meek and gentle in heart (Matthew 11:29).

The one group which bears some similarity with Jesus is that group of *Sign Prophets* who arose AD 44-70, the best known of whom are Theudas and the Egyptian prophet for whom the apostle Paul was mistaken in Jerusalem in AD 57 (Acts 21:38). Information about these prophets can be found in Josephus and the New Testament. These men have it in common that they were self-styled prophets who led a multitude to the Jordan, to the wilderness, to the walls of Jerusalem, to the temple (or some other place which had been significant in Israel's salvation history) where they promised them some sign from which, they said, "salvation" or "freedom" would follow. (It should be noted that none of these prophets succeeded in performing the signs they promised.)

Jesus also once led a multitude to the wilderness where he performed the sign of the loaves, where he was hailed as the long awaited Prophet (John 6:1-15). But Jesus preceded the first of these sign prophets by fifteen years, so they cannot have provided the group or movement to whom he may be linked. Quite the reverse, in fact; these prophets may well have been influenced by Jesus and his well-known sign in the wilderness. It is significant that "John [the Baptist] did no sign" (John 10:41), so that the Sign Prophets were not influenced by him. No other prophetic figure known to us performed signs during or before the ministry of Jesus.

Our argument, therefore, is that Jesus cannot be neatly slotted into any of the socio-religious pigeon holes of that time—as witnessed by the failure of the scholars to agree precisely who he was. In sum we may say that though a Jew, Jesus is distinct from any of the known groups within Judaism at the time. While gladly acknowledging his

Jewishness it is right that the verdict of history has placed him above contemporary racial constraints.

Jesus, knew his teachings to be distinctive, to be new. Jesus was questioned why his disciples did not fast, whereas the disciples of the Baptist and of the Pharisees did fast. In response he told two parables—the Unshrunk Patch and the New Wine (Mark 2:21–22). The coat and the wineskins are "old," outmoded; they represent Judaism. The patch and the wine are "unshrunk" and "new" respectively and they stand for Jesus' teaching. Jesus' teaching is different in kind to the existing teachings of Judaism. They cannot be merely "added" to Judaism for they will destroy it just as a piece of unshrunk cloth will destroy the coat on to which it is patched and new wine will destroy the old wineskins into which it is poured. In other words, Judaism and Jesus will not mix; they are different not similar. History has proved Jesus' words correct; Christianity was to "tear away" from Judaism.

What is this teaching of Jesus that is so radically new? His "new" teaching consists of two things, in fact, though they are so closely related as to be two sides of the one coin.

On one hand, he is referring to his proclamation that God's *kingdom* is imminent, whereupon when they heard it, the people in the synagogue in Capernaum declared it to be a "new teaching" different from that of the Pharisees (Mark 1:27).

On the other hand, on the eve of his death Jesus instituted a *new covenant*, which would be by means of his "blood" or death (Luke 22:20).

Kingdom and covenant are both new. The former relates to God and his rule, the latter to the covenant people now ruled by God. Both kingdom and covenant are mediated by Jesus. They arise out of and fulfil the Old Testament; but in the process they also dispense with the old covenant, of which the Judaism of Jesus' day was the historical expression. Jesus' twin parables of newness—the Unshrunk Patch and the New Wine—aptly demonstrate the discontinuity of Jesus with Judaism.

CHARISMATIC LEADERS CONTEMPORARY WITH JESUS

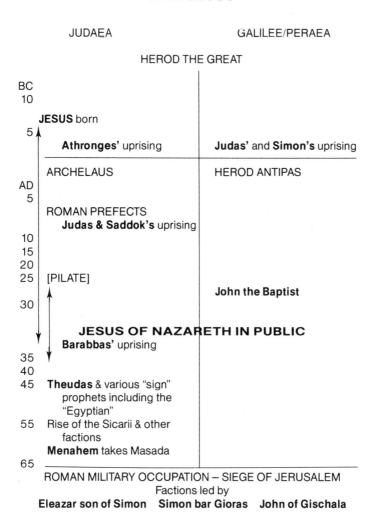

JUDAEA	GALILEE/PERAEA

HEROD THE GREAT

BC
10

JESUS born

5

Athronges' uprising   **Judas'** and **Simon's** uprising

ARCHELAUS   HEROD ANTIPAS

AD
5

ROMAN PREFECTS
Judas & Saddok's uprising

10
15
20
25   [PILATE]

                                  John the Baptist

30

        JESUS OF NAZARETH IN PUBLIC
        Barabbas' uprising

35
40
45   **Theudas** & various "sign"
      prophets including the
      "Egyptian"
55   Rise of the Sicarii & other
      factions
      Menahem takes Masada

65

ROMAN MILITARY OCCUPATION – SIEGE OF JERUSALEM
Factions led by
Eleazar son of Simon   Simon bar Gioras   John of Gischala

70   FALL OF JERUSALEM AND DESTRUCTION OF TEMPLE

Further reading:

M.J. Borg, *Conflict, Holiness and Politics in the Teachings of Jesus,* (New York and Toronto, Edwin Mellen Press, 1984)

S.G.F. Brandon, *Jesus and the Zealots,* (Manchester, University Press, 1967)

M. Hengel, *The Charismatic Leader and His Followers,* (Edinburgh, Clark, 1981)

J. Riches, *Jesus and the Transformation of Judaism,* (London, Darton, Longman and Todd, 1980)

E.P. Sanders, *Jesus and Judaism,* (London, SCM Press, 1984)

L. Swidler, "Contemporary Implications of the Jewish-Christian Dialogue on Jesus Christ", *Dialogue and Alliance* 2/3 (1988) pp.95–108

G. Vermes, *Jesus the Jew,* (London, Collins, 1973)

M. Wilcox, "Jesus in the Light of His Jewish Environment", *Aufstieg und Niedergang der römischen Welt,* ii, (1982), pp.131–195

N.T. Wright, "Jesus, Israel and the Cross", *The Society of Biblical Literature Seminar Papers,* 1985, pp.70–95

5 A MOVEMENT WITH A DIFFERENCE

Though an authentic figure of Jewish history, Jesus is also "new", distinctive. This is confirmed by the distinctive movement established by him.

We now take a step forward from the person of Jesus to consider the movement established by him. What kind of movement was it that issued from the Nazarene, Jesus?

Writing in the mid fifties the Apostle Paul commented on the rapid growth of the movement. He refers to it as a spreading, abundantly fruiting vine. (Colossians 1:6; cf. Romans 10:18). In the mid sixties Peter wrote to Christians throughout the provinces of Pontus, Galatia, Asia and Bithynia about their "brotherhood throughout the world" (1 Peter 5:9; 2:17). Early in the second century Roman authors like Pliny, Tacitus and Suetonius likened it to a rapidly spreading disease.

There were other movements in first century Palestine. One has only to think of the Pharisees, the Sadducees, the Qumran Covenanters, the *Sicarii*, the Zealots and those who followed the Sign Prophets, to be reminded of just a few groups which were active at or near the time of Jesus.

There are two major differences, however, between these movements and the Jesus-Movement.

First, the other movements mentioned were strictly confined to the Jewish people. Within five years of Jesus' crucifixion the Jesus-movement had begun to spread from the Jews to the Gentiles. Cornelius, a Roman centurion stationed at Caesarea Maritima, and his family were baptized in c. 37 (Acts 10).

Second, the other movements were all directed towards the cause of Israel and God's dealings with his chosen people. Some leaders were preoccupied with religion and purity, others with military liberation. But, whatever it was, the movement only gave expression to the interchangeable realities that Israel was both a political entity and a people conscious that they were God's chosen people. Religion and political action were merely different expressions of the one reality: Yahweh was their God and they were his people.

The leadership of the groups was important—rabbis like ben Zakkai, sign prophets like Theudas or the Egyptian prophet or military leaders like Menahem, leader of the *Sicarii* gave their movements direction and character. They were all preoccupied with the one great cause—the deliverance of God's holy nation from the Gentiles. The leaders were not followed purely on account of their personal charisma or for the sake of personal loyalty to them. The leaders only served to bring the cause of God's elect people into sharp focus.

By contrast, those who belonged to the Jesus-movement were devoted to him personally, whether Jews or Gentiles. They belonged to the movement for no other reason than their personal adherence to Jesus. The cause of Jesus was greater than the cause of Israel. To illustrate: when war broke out between Romans and Jews in 66, the Jerusalem church, although composed exclusively of Jews, withdrew from Judaea and took no part in the war. Christian Jews had no military allegiance to their nation's cause, which was the cause of Yahweh.

Pliny, legate of Bithynia told the emperor Trajan early in the second century that the Christians "met regularly before dawn on a fixed day to chant verses alternately among themselves in honour of Christ as if to a god" (*Epistle* 10:96.7). In his examination of them Pliny required those who had been arrested publicly to "revile the name of Christ", something he said "I understand [no] genuine Christian can be induced to do". Pliny leaves us in no doubt that this movement was made up of people who had a life and death devotion to Christ, whom together they worshipped as a god.

This is confirmed by the strange sounding Aramaic words embedded in the Greek text at the end of Paul's first letter to the Corinthians. The words *Marana tha* mean "Come, O Lord" (16:22) and they echo the earliest Christians' worship of Jesus in Jerusalem in their original Aramaic dialect. They called Jesus *mara*, "Lord", in worship of him. Paul encourages his readers in the Greek speaking churches to "sing and make melody to the [*kyrios* =] the Lord" (Ephesians 5:19).

No other Palestinian movement-leader of the time was worshipped, whether during his lifetime or after his death. The only person among the Jews of the time known to have accepted worship was King Agrippa, who was struck down in 44 in Caesarea Maritima at the very moment he was declared to be a god. Agrippa died a few days later, as both Jewish and Christian sources narrate with fierce pleasure (*Josephus, Jewish Antiquities* xix.345; Acts 12:22-23).

Jesus, however, was worshipped at gatherings of the movement. Hymns of praise to Jesus were composed and some of these have survived in quotation within the letters of Paul (e.g. Philippians 2:5-11).

Joining the movement was by means of the rite of baptism, at which the new member confessed to all present that, "Jesus Christ is Lord" (1 Corinthians 12:3,13) . This person was said to have been "baptized into Christ" (Galatians 3:27). The body of believers was spoken of as "the body" or even as "Christ"(1 Corinthians 12:12); members were known as "members of Christ" (1 Corinthians 6:15) who have "put on Christ" (Galatians 3:27) and who have "learned Christ" (Ephesians 4:20). The "body of Christ" (1 Corinthians 12:27) was to be controlled by "the mind of Christ" (Philippians 2:5).

When the members of the movement met they "remembered" their Lord's last meal with his disciples in the breaking of bread at "the table of the Lord", the sharing of "the cup of the Lord" and the quotation of the words Jesus spoke on the evening he was betrayed (1 Corinthians 10:19; 11:23-26). Their belief-credos were focused on Jesus.

Paul reminded the Thessalonians in his first letter, written
to them in 50, that:

We believe

that	Jesus	died
[that	Jesus]	rose again
that with	[Jesus] God will	bring those who have fallen asleep

(4:15; cf. Romans 9:9)

Within the movement the words of Jesus had only to be
quoted on a subject on which he had spoken and that was
an end of the matter, as for example in the question of the
permanency of marriage (1 Corinthians 7:10–11).

Appeal was made repeatedly to Jesus' characteristic grace,
gentleness, meekness, humility, kindness to outsiders, concern
for the lost and his non-vindictive demeanour at the time
of his death as a point of imitation by members of the
movement (2 Corinthians 8:9; 10:1; Philippians 2:5–11;
Romans 15:7; 1 Corinthians 11:1; 1 Peter 2:22–23). In its
moral and ethical life the community of believers was to
embody the behaviour of Jesus. Husbands were to model
their relationship to their wives on Christ's relationship with
the church (Ephesians 5:22–33).

Peter wrote to his readers that "without having seen [Jesus
Christ] you love him"; they were to "reverence Christ [in their
hearts] as Lord" (1 Peter 1:8; 3:14).

Jesus was to be the only and absolute point of
commitment of the members of this movement. Paul
encouraged the believers in Colossae, "As therefore you have
received Christ Jesus the Lord, so live in him, rooted and
built up in him..." (2:6)

Moreover, in their promotional activities, the members
of the movement did not invite outsiders to join the
movement, in the first instance, but to commit themselves
in life and death loyalty to the *Lord* Jesus. The movement
did not offer a program of political or social reform. Jesus
was the sole focus of interest. The Acts of the Apostles tersely
describes Philip the Evangelist speaking to the Ethiopian "he
told him the good news: *Jesus*" (Acts 8:35 cf. 4,5). The gospel
message could be simply described as "concerning [God's]
Son" (Romans 1:3 cf. 2 Corinthians 1:19).

Unlike other movements of the time this movement had only one reason for existence—its founder, Jesus. Jesus was the focus of attention when members met and the focus of conversation with outsiders.

The distinctive nature of the Jesus-movement confirms our observation that its founder, Jesus, was also distinctive.

Further reading:

M. Hengel, *Acts and the History of Earliest Christianity*, (London, SCM, 1979)

C.F.D. Moule, *The Birth of the New Testament*, (London, A. & C. Black, 1973)

V.E. Neufeld, *The Earliest Christian Confessions*, (Leiden, Brill, 1963)

R.L. Wilken, *The Christians as the Romans Saw Them*, (Yale University Press, New Haven, 1984)

6 THE FILIAL FACE AND THE PUBLIC FACE

It is of utmost importance that we relate to Jesus in terms of his two-sidedness, that we see both his faces, but in particular his filial face. The people at large saw only the public face—which some New Quest scholars also see. But the Twelve saw both faces.

We return to consider Jesus further, in particular his two-sidedness.

Jesus' early ministry in Galilee, as recorded in the Gospel of Mark, is helpful in defining Jesus' public face. At the beginning of Mark's narrative he appears as a teacher in the synagogues of Galilee (Mark 1:21,39). When he took the scroll of a prophet and taught from it (Luke 4:16–21), those present in the synagogue would have recognised him as a rabbi. Indeed he is usually addressed as "Rabbi" (Mark 9:5; 10:51; 11:21; 14:45), or its equivalent, "Teacher" (Mark 4:38; 9:17,38; 10:17,20,35; 12:14,19,32; 13:1) and spoken of as such (Mark 5:35; 10:35; 14:14). Nicodemus addressed Jesus as "Rabbi,...you are a teacher come from God" (John 3:2).

This definition of Jesus is also to be found in the Jewish historian Josephus. Writing at the close of the first century Josephus calls Jesus "a wise man...a teacher" (*Jewish Antiquities* xviii,63). Later Jewish writings speak of Jesus as one who "led Israel astray and enticed them into apostasy"

(*Sanhedrin* 43a). This sentiment reflects the bitterness which developed between Jews and Christians in the centuries after Christ. But a faint memory of Jesus as a rabbi may still be detected in this comment. We can understand why some New Quest scholars (e.g. Vermes, Wilcox) classify Jesus, however broadly and with whatever qualifications, as a Jewish rabbi, a sage.

On the other hand, those who heard him might just as easily have concluded that he was a prophet. Indeed Jesus' public message of the nearness of God's Kingdom was a close continuation of John the Baptist's (Mark 1:14-15; cf. Matthew 3:2). His public message, whether in exposition of the prophets in the synagogues or by means of parables to the crowds in the open, focused on the announcement of the approaching kingdom of God and the call to repentance. There is good reason to believe that it was as a prophet that the people of the time recognised him (John 6:14; Mark 6:14-15; 8:28). Those New Quest scholars (e.g. Sanders, Horsley & Hanson) who prefer to see Jesus in this role have good reason for doing so.

We can see therefore how the Galileans in the synagogues and in the public places, would have identified Jesus as a rabbi or a prophet and perhaps even fleetingly as a zealot (cf. John 2:18). The New Quest scholars stand in the shoes of Jesus' Jewish contemporaries; they stand where those Jews stood and see the Jewish face of Jesus—as a rabbi or a prophet.

Nonetheless these were immediate, even superficial impressions of Jesus. The teachings of Jesus must be analysed—in the synagogues and to the crowds, and more particularly to the Twelve. Whereas the rabbis quoted from the judgements of other teachers (Mark 1:22; 7:4-8), Jesus spoke on his own authority, introducing his teaching with "Amen, I say to you" (e.g. Mark 1:22; 3:28). Jesus, therefore, cannot be thought of as a rabbi in other than a general sense; he is different from other rabbis. Certainly there is no surviving evidence that the earliest Christians venerated Jesus as a rabbi.

If there were similarities between Jesus and John the Baptist, there were also differences. John was an ascetic, whose disciples practised fasting; Jesus was called "a glutton and a drunkard" and his disciples did not fast (Matthew 11:19; Mark 2:18-19). John did not perform miracle signs, whereas Jesus did (John 10:41).

It is true that for a brief period the earliest Christians regarded Jesus as a prophet. However he was no ordinary prophet resembling John the Baptist or Theudas but the long-awaited prophet like Moses spoken of in Deuteronomy 18:15-19. This was not a prophet, but *the* prophet whom the people would obey. This was a Moses-Messiah, a new leader of God's people. Both Peter and Stephen proclaimed Jesus as this mighty prophet (Acts 3:22-23; 7:37). It is curious, therefore, that this presentation of Jesus did not continue. Vermes (p.99) may be correct in his suggestion that the rise of prophets like Theudas in the forties, whose style was reminiscent of Moses or Joshua, may have deterred the early Christians from referring to Jesus as the prophet like Moses. In any case the opinion of Peter and Stephen that Jesus was this Moses-like prophet did not rest on the popular identification of Jesus as a prophet.

Our argument is that we must draw a distinction between how Jesus was perceived by the people at large and how, over a period of time, he came to be perceived by the Twelve. In the perception of the Jewish people, a perception now expressed by some New Quest scholars, Jesus was seen to have the face of a rabbi or prophet. In the perception of the Twelve, however, Jesus came also to have another face, a filial face. It is this filial face, as seen by the Twelve, which in particular comes to be expressed first in the early preaching and then in the writings which compose the New Testament and ultimately in the creeds of the church.

It is for this reason Christians today must insist on the two-sidedness of Jesus. Along with New Quest scholars we affirm his genuine humanity as a Jew of the first century. But equally we affirm him as the Son of God. This complete two-sided understanding was not the perception of the people in general but of the Twelve, from whom it has come to us through the New Testament to the church creeds.

According to Mark, Jesus called four fishermen in the first instance to leave their occupations and follow him as his disciples (1:16–20). A fifth man, Levi the customs collector, was then called into Jesus' day to day company (2:13–14). At this time Jesus was also teaching in the synagogues and also (1:21–28,39), as his disputes with the Pharisees forced him from the synagogues, he began to teach in the open— chiefly by the lakeside (2:13; 3:7–12; 4:1–2). Jesus then called a further seven men, making twelve in all, who left their occupations to be with him as his pupils. As such Jesus related to them on the model of a rabbi to his pupils.

There were differences, however. Rabbis usually had just a few students who approached the teacher to learn from him. Rabbi Jesus, however, took the initiative and called not a few, but twelve disciples. Moreover, he did not appeal to the authority of other teachers before him.

Soon after his calling of the Twelve Jesus devoted himself to them, with only occasional contacts with the great crowds (4:1; 6:34; 8:1) and with the sick and diseased. By his teaching he prepared them for their mission to Galilee and ultimately for their mission to all Israel and beyond that to the nations.

It was in the intimacy of fellowship with the Twelve that Jesus revealed his filial relationship with God, his mission to Israel and the nations and the future of the Son of Man. Jesus taught the multitudes by parables that the kingdom of God was imminent. But he revealed the mystery of the kingdom of God to the Twelve, not to people in general (Mark 4:10–12,34). Jesus does not reveal himself to the Twelve as a prophet, but as the Son of Man who is the Son of God and the Servant of the Lord.

To the multitudes, however, Jesus remained as mystifying as they found his parables to be. It is Jesus' teaching to the Twelve, which has influenced the thinking of the New Testament and ultimately the creeds. The New Quest scholars who stand in the shoes of the Jewish multitudes of the period and see only the public face of Jesus—Jesus the rabbi or prophet. To that extent their understanding of Jesus is external and, indeed, "one-sided".

Jesus distinguishes between the perception of the people at large and the Twelve. The "secret of the kingdom of God" is given to the Twelve but to those on the outside there is no comprehension (Mark 4:11-12). The first three soils in the Parable reject the seed; only the good soil (= those Jesus has called) produce crops for harvesting at the end (Mark 4:3-8). Jesus hides the filial relationship he has with God from the wise and learned (the religious leaders and those who follow them) and reveals it to little children (the Twelve and others close to Jesus) (Matthew 11:25-27). Flesh and blood—the ordinary perception of Jesus—does not reveal to Peter that Jesus is the Christ, the Son of the Living God, but only the Father in heaven (Matthew 16:16-17).

Thus the Twelve did not invent the notion that Jesus was the Son of God. It came from Jesus who revealed his filial relationship to the Twelve, and it was made clear to them by God. To the Galileans of the period who observed him, however, Jesus remained a rabbi, a prophet of the kingdom of God—an oblique character who taught mystifying parables and cast out demons. The New Quest scholars, while displaying enviable historical expertise remain at arm's length from Jesus; he is for them what he was for those Galileans.

Where, therefore, did Jesus' own filial consciousness originate? Doubtless Jesus' own study of the scriptures played a major part in the formation of his thinking. Nonetheless, we are not able to say with confidence where Jesus' sense of his identity came from—except that it appears to have been well developed in the twelve-year-old boy in the temple who spoke of the house of Yahweh as "my father's house" (Luke 2:49). Years later, the heavenly voice assuring him that he was "my beloved son" at the time of the baptism was probably remembered as a major confirmation of his identity as the Son (Luke 3:21-22)—something that was put to a severe test in the wilderness incident that followed (Luke 4:3,9).

Thus Jesus has two faces—the public face seen by Galileans of the time (which New Quest scholars through their historical researches also see) and the other, filial face, which he revealed to the Twelve.

Public face	← JESUS →	*Filial face*
To the Galileans		To the Twelve—
—and the New		and the New
Quest:		Testament: Jesus,
Jesus is Rabbi		the Son of Man
and/or Prophet.		is Son of God
His essential		and Servant. His
identity is hidden		essential identity
		is revealed

The chain of revelation—that Jesus is the Son—from God to Jesus, from Jesus to the Twelve, from the Twelve to the world, may also be expressed as a progression:

GOD → JESUS	JESUS → THE TWELVE	TWELVE → THE WORLD
(The Baptism)	(From call to Pentecost)	(In the New Testament)

It is clear from the above that historical research alone can only go so far in identifying Jesus of Nazareth. Historical enquiry into Jesus and his times cannot penetrate beyond the recognition that he was some kind of rabbi or prophet, a genuine figure of the Judaism of the day. But it is only as we stand in the shoes of the Twelve, that is within the structures of thought of the New Testament, that we can get beyond the one-sided public impression of Jesus, to see his filial face.

But can we trust the writers of the New Testament? I have argued in *Is the New Testament History?* that what these nine authors write is historical in character, that they can take their place with other historical writers of the period on whom we depend for reliable information from the period. These authors handle historical data in a responsible way.

As to the rightness of their insight into Jesus—that he was the Son of God—we may point to the historical evidence for the resurrection and the rise of early Christianity. But in the end those who read the New Testament must come to their own conclusions, measuring Jesus by their own moral and spiritual values. As many have discovered, however, this is a disturbing two-way experience. As we read about Jesus we have the painful sense that Someone is reading us. In evaluating Jesus we sense that it is we who are being evaluated.

Further reading:
P.W. Barnett, *Is the New Testament History?* (Sydney, Hodder and Stoughton, 1984)
M. Hengel, *The Charismatic Leader and his Followers*, (Edinburgh, T. & T. Clark, 1981)

7 The Mission of Jesus

*While Jesus' immediate mission was to Israel, he looked
beyond his own people to the Nations; his mission was
to both. Jesus' mission was to create a multi-ethnic
people of God, which would grow out of the Twelve.*

The mission of Jesus was only dimly perceived by the people
at large, and therefore is not remembered by them in their
historical literature. The Twelve and those with them who
were close to Jesus, however, were taught what it was that
Jesus had come to do. Soon the understanding of the Twelve
would find expression in the early preaching and then in the
literature flowing from it—the New Testament.

It is to be regretted that Jesus' mission is usually
considered independently of his movements, and what we
might call the geographical structure of his ministry. This
is due in the main to the hitherto prevailing scepticism about
establishing a sequence and chronology for Jesus. In our
view, scholars have adopted a too minimal view of the
historical component of the Gospels. Following J.A.T.
Robinson, *The Priority of John*, a more positive attitude
has been taken in what follows.

Robinson has shown that the references to Jewish feasts
in the Gospel of John are especially helpful in establishing
a time-frame for Jesus' ministry. John mentions three
Passovers (2:23; 6:4; 12:1), which always occur in the spring,
as well as a Feast of Tabernacles (7:2) and a Feast of
Dedication (10:22) which fall in autumn and mid-winter
respectively. (Although scholars generally do not use the

Gospel of John in establishing the structure of Jesus' ministry Robinson makes a good case for doing so).

Mark is less helpful in establishing the passage of time. He does, however, mention three moments of time: the plucking of grain (2:23), which would have occurred in spring/summer; the "green grass" on which the multitude sat (6:39), which would indicate winter/spring and the Passover at which Jesus was arrested (14:12).

Despite the considerable differences of subject matter between John and Mark there are five important reference points in common:

		JOHN	MARK
1	John's baptism of Jesus	1:32–33	1:9–11
2	John's imprisonment/	3:24	1:14–15
	Jesus' mission to Galilee	4:3,43,47	
3	Jesus feeds the multitude	6:1–15	6:30–45
4	Jesus leaves Galilee for Judaea	7:9–10	10:1
5	Jesus' arrival in Jerusalem	12:1f	11:11

Also in common between John and Mark is that each devotes the greater part of his Gospel to the last year of Jesus' life—that is between the Passover at which he fed the multitude and the Passover at which he met his death. Both of them squeeze the earlier part of Jesus' ministry, which lasted more than three years, into only five chapters.

Based on the Gospels of John and Mark, the structure of Jesus' public ministry may be reconstructed as follows:

Phase 1: 29 Peraea: Jesus baptized by John
            Galilee: Jesus returns for a period
         30 Jerusalem: Jesus at Passover (Spring)
            Samaria: Jesus' brief ministry
            (Arrest of John the Baptist)

Phase 2: 31 Galilee: Mission of Jesus (Summer)
         31 Galilee: Mission of the Twelve (Summer)
         32 Galilee: Jesus feeds multitude (Spring)

Phase 3: 32 Fugitive in the west, east & north of
            Galilee (Spring/Summer)

32 Jerusalem, Peraea, Judaea
    (Autumn/Winter)
33 Jerusalem: Executed at Passover (Spring)

Thus there were three phases in the ministry of Jesus.

The first phase was between Jesus' baptism and the arrest of John the Baptist, when his ministry was semi-public. Jesus did not step out into the full blaze of public life until John was removed from the scene.

The second was between the arrest of John the Baptist and the feeding of the multitude in Galilee. Jesus proclaimed his message in public, both in the synagogues and in the open to great crowds in Galilee. During this period he instructed the Twelve for their mission to the towns of Galilee.

The final phase of Jesus' ministry was between the feeding incident and his execution. The attempt to make him "king" in Galilee (John 6:15) meant that thereafter Jesus was forced to travel in secret in territories beyond the reach of Antipas, the tetrarch of Galilee. Jesus finally moved from Galilee to Jerusalem. This final year of Jesus' ministry was mostly directed to private teaching of the Twelve.

We have given this outline of Jesus' ministry in some detail in the conviction that significant sequences of Jesus' public ministry are historically recoverable. In our view Bultmann was overly sceptical about the historical recoverability of Jesus' ministry.

On the other hand, the New Quest scholars, though arguing for a greater knowledge about Jesus tend to ignore the question of the geographical structure of Jesus' ministry. In common with most scholars they tend to treat Jesus' teachings separately from their context in his public ministry. But if there is a structure, a plan that Jesus was working to, then many of his sayings and teachings will be seen to make sense and to have special significance depending where and when they occur within that structure. For example, Jesus' teachings about his death and the second advent of the Son of Man mostly occur in the twelve-month period between the Feeding of the Multitude and the final Passover when he was based in or near Jerusalem.

MAP 2:
THE THREE PHASES OF JESUS' MINISTRY

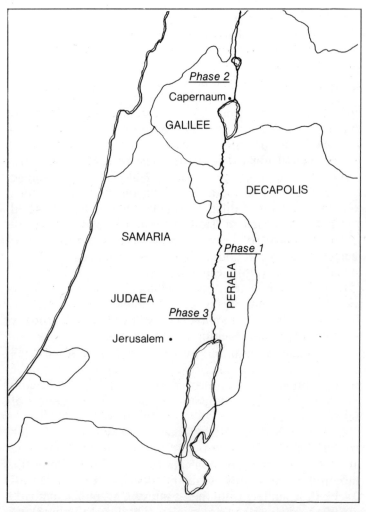

Phase 1: Concurrent with John the Baptist. Baptised by John the Baptist in Peraea, returns to Galilee, goes to Jerusalem for Passover, then to Samaria (John 1–4).
Phase 2: From arrest of John the Baptist to feeding of the 5000. Teaches in synagogues centred in Capernaum, then in open and in the Decapolis. Mission of the Twelve and feeding of the 5000 ends Phase 2 (Mark 1–6).
Phase 3: From feeding of the 5000 to the crucifixion. Fugitive from Herod Antipas, tetrarch of Galilee. Travels in west, east and north, until his final visit to the south arriving in Jerusalem six days before Passover (John 7–20; Mark 7–16).

What were Jesus' aims?

These are known primarily from the sayings of Jesus recorded in the Gospels. Nonetheless, Jesus took certain actions which were so deliberate as to suggest they were part of some strategy on his part. In particular we note:

Jesus' *prophecy* of the destruction of the temple near the beginning of his ministry, probably accompanied by some *action of clearing* the temple (John 2:1-19)

Jesus' *casting out of demons* at the time of his proclamation of the kingdom of God (Mark 1)

Jesus' *table fellowship* with moral outcasts and *healing* of the diseased (Mark 1-2)

Jesus' choice of *Twelve* disciples soon after his commencement of activities in Galilee (Mark 3:13-14)

Jesus' *feeding* of the multitude in the wilderness at Passover time, after the mission of the Twelve to Galilee (Mark 6:31-45/John 6:1-14)

Jesus' public and mounted *entry* to Jerusalem at the next Passover (Mark 11:1-10/John 12:12-19)

Jesus' dramatic *clearing of the temple*, followed by further prophecy of the destruction of the temple (Mark 11:15-19; 13:1-23)

These deliberate and public actions signify that Jesus was very purposeful in relationship to the people of Israel. The actions on their own, however, leave uncertain exactly what his purposes were. The words of Jesus must be studied to interpret the meaning of the actions.

Jesus' words indeed reveal him to have been a man with a deep sense of mission. He had a profound consciousness of being sent by God:

Whoever receives me receives him who sent me (Mark 9:37)

[God]...had...a beloved son; finally he sent him (Mark 12:6)

Jesus was convinced he was God's beloved Son, "sent" by God, as God's apostle, with a definite purpose.

Closely related to his "sent" sayings are Jesus' oft-repeated statements of purpose: "I came to" or "I came that". Jesus came because he was sent by God to fulfil a particular mission. For example he said:

> I came...that I may proclaim [the Kingdom of God] (Mark 1:38,15)

> I came...to call...sinners (Mark 2:17)

> The Son of man came to seek and to save the lost (Luke 19:10)

> I came ...to cast a fire upon the earth (Luke 12:49)

> The Son of man came...to give his life a ransom for many (Mark 10:45)

If Jesus was such a man of purpose, what was that purpose? What did he "come" to do? What mission had God "sent" him to fulfil? Is there some way we can make sense out these apparently unrelated statements of intention?

As we study the sayings of Jesus a pattern of thought emerges, a set of aims, that take us by surprise. Jesus' aims and purpose are overwhelmingly in relation to God's kingdom or reign over a covenant people. That in itself is no surprise. Nor are we surprised that God's kingdom will be applied to his people Israel.

What is so unexpected is that Jesus' "kingdom" aims are as connected as they are to Israel, on one hand, *and* to the the Nations (= Gentiles), on the other. So far as we know Jesus is unique among the religious and political leaders in that he alone spoke of the salvation of the Nations; for every other group-leader the Nations were the enemies of God and of God's people. In their desire to locate Jesus within the context of first century Judaism the New Quest scholars tend to play down or reject the view that Jesus saw the salvation of the Nations as fundamental to his mission.

But there is also good evidence that Jesus saw himself involved in a two-stage mission. The first stage was directed exclusively to *Israel*. He states explicitly, "I was sent only to the lost sheep of the house of Israel" (Matthew 15:24). In the mission of the Twelve he directed them, "Go nowhere among the Gentiles and enter no town of the Samaritans, but go rather to the lost sheep of the house of Israel" (Matthew 10:5).

When Jesus was travelling inside the borders of Tyre and Sidon, a Gentile woman asked him to cast the demon from her daughter. He replied, "Let the children [= people of Israel] first be fed, for it is not right to take the children's bread and feed it to dogs [= the Gentiles]" (Mark 7:27).

The second stage of Jesus' mission, however, would be directed to the *Nations* (= Gentiles), whose in-gathering was dependent upon and subsequent to his ransom-death, which would be "for many" (Mark 10:45; 14:24.) In biblical thought "many" includes the Nations (See Isaiah 52:15; cf. 52:14; 53:11,12).

Jesus foresaw that the mission to Israel would, in large measure, fail whereas the response of the Nations would be infinitely greater.

This Israel-Nations theme occurs many times in the sayings of Jesus, as the following three examples show.

First, in the incident in Capernaum where the *Gentile* Centurion asks only that Jesus speak a word of healing for his servant, Jesus comments, "Truly, I say to you, not even in Israel have I found such faith."

Jesus then adds,

I tell you, many will come from east and west and sit at table with Abraham, Isaac and Jacob in the kingdom of heaven, while the sons of the kingdom will be thrown into outer darkness; there men will weep and gnash their teeth (Matthew 8:11-12).

The Gentile in Capernaum was a forerunner of the "many" Gentiles who would stream into the great banquet of the kingdom of heaven attended by the patriarchs of Israel, a banquet at which the sons of the kingdom, the people of Israel, would find no place.

Second, in the Parable of the King's Wedding Banquet for his son (Matthew 22:1-10) those initially invited [= Israel] not only declined the king's invitation, they mistreated and killed the king's servants who issued the invitations. Since the banquet was ready the king directed his servants to bring others [= the Nations] into the banquet hall.

Third, speaking in the synagogue in Nazareth, Jesus drew

attention to the greater response of Gentiles in times past, to the prophets Elijah and Elisha respectively.

But in truth, I tell you, there were many widows in Israel in the days of Elijah, when the heaven was shut up three years and six months...and Elijah was sent to none of them but only to Zarephath, in the land of Sidon, to a woman who was a widow. And there were many lepers in Israel in the time of the prophet Elisha; and none of them was cleansed, but only Naaman the Syrian (Luke 4:25-29).

Clearly Jesus anticipated a greater response from the Gentiles than from Israel.

Many of the sayings of Jesus reflect the failure of Israel to respond to his mission. Consider, for example, the Parable of the Fig Tree which expresses the patience of Jesus in the face of a stony response:

A man had a fig tree planted in his vineyard; and he came seeking fruit on it and found none. And he said to the vinedresser, 'Lo. these three years I have come seeking fruit on this fig tree, and I find none. Cut it down. Why should it use up the ground?' And he answered him, 'Let it alone, sir, this year also, till I dig about it and put on manure. And if it bears fruit next year well and good; but if not you can cut it down.' (Luke 13:6-9)

Israel's time to respond to Jesus is limited. When Jesus came finally to Jerusalem, finding no repentance he cursed a fig tree, a symbol of Israel, and it died (Mark 11:12-14; 20-25). Israel's time of opportunity had now passed. It was for that reason Jesus wept over the city, and said,

O Jerusalem, Jerusalem, killing the prophets and stoning those who are sent to you! How often would I have gathered your children together as a hen gathers her brood under her wings, and you would not. Behold your house is forsaken and desolate. For I tell you, you will not see me again until you say, 'Blessed is he who comes in the name of the Lord' (Matthew 23:37-39).

According to Jesus he is "the stone which the builders [= the leaders of Israel] rejected" which, nonetheless, "has become the capstone; the Lord has done this, and it is marvellous in our eyes" (Mark 12:10).

Why did Israel reject Jesus' mission? In brief terms, it was because of Israel's national pride, her sense of superiority. Were they not Abraham's children, God's holy people to whom God's Anointed One would come, with the great temple of God standing in their midst?

Various groups and factions gave expression to the aspirations of Israel, but religious triumphalism lay at the heart of them all. The two, closely-related movements in Israel, which claimed greatest support, the "Pharisees", a purity-orientated religious sect, and the "Fourth Philosophy", a nationalistic military movement, had aims and values which were utterly opposed to those of Jesus. The Sermon on the Mount (Matthew 5-7) explicitly contradicts their teachings (See my *Bethlehem to Patmos*, pp.108–117).

Jesus, however, addressed the people not in terms which encouraged racial and religious pride, but in terms of their real poverty before God, as a people "lost" from God. Hence the "beatitudes" call upon the hearers to acknowledge their deep need before God. Without that acknowledgement God's kingdom would not rest upon them. Those who "laboured" and were "heavily laden" by the oppressive injustice of the times were invited to come for "rest" (an end-time blessing) not to a military messiah but to One who was "gentle and lowly in heart" (Matthew 11:29). Unlike the followers of the revolutionary leaders of the time Jesus' people were not called upon to be "violent" but to be to be "little", "child"-like (Matthew 11:11–12). Both the master who called in humility and meekness, and the demands of his call were in stark contrast with the nationalism and triumphalism of other groups in Israel at that time.

Jesus' announcement to Israel was dramatically embodied in his relationships with people in desperate circumstances. He healed the demon-possessed, the diseased, the disabled— needy folk who, significantly, were excluded from the desert covenant-community at Qumran. There was no place there for the physically or morally blemished. But Jesus ate (a sacred and eschatological gesture) with tax collectors and whores—people despised by the Pharisees for their immorality and disobedience to the Torah. It was bitterly complained that he "received sinners and ate with them"

(Luke 15:1) and that he was "a friend of tax collectors and sinners" (Matthew 11:19).

But such folk were the "lost sheep of the house of Israel" whom he had been sent to seek and to save. These were the "sick" whom the Physician had come to heal. Jesus remarked, with respect to the tax collector Zacchaeus of Jericho, a man despised within his community that, "...he also is a son of Abraham. For the Son of man came to seek and to save the lost" (Luke 19:9–10).

Zacchaeus was a lost sheep in Israel whom Jesus sought and saved, as expressed by sitting at table in the tax collector's house. But this call of Jesus greatly offended the leaders of the people and led them to repudiate Jesus' mission to Israel.

What, then, was Jesus' announcement to Israel?

Jesus announced that the kingdom or reign of God had dawned (by means of his proclamation and the casting out of demons). In response the people of Israel were called upon to repent, that is to return to their God (Mark 1:14–15).

Jesus saw himself as the last of the prophetic messengers God would send to his chosen people. Previous servants of God had been mishandled and killed by the people. But "[God] still had one other [servant], a beloved son; finally he sent him to them, saying, 'They will respect my son' " (Mark 12:6).

The great majority of the people of Israel, however, did not recognise the beloved Son God sent to them. Only the Twelve had the glimmerings of understanding about Jesus' filial relationship with God. When requested by the scribes to give a "sign" that the messianic age had drawn near (e.g. by some freakish manifestation), Jesus replied that no "sign" would be given except that of the prophet Jonah. Like Jonah and the succession of the prophets of God, Jesus preached repentance. Repentance would be the only "sign" God would give to Israel that the end-times had come (Matthew 12:39–41/Luke 11:29–32).

Jesus' action in feeding the multitude is full of pathos. Here is the shepherd king of Israel teaching and feeding his people in a messianic setting. The people, however, are happy to be fed but not to be taught, as the long discourse in John 6:25-65 makes plain. Their attempted imposition on him of a nationalistic kingship symbolizes their failure to comprehend his true identity (John 6:14-15, 26).

According to Jesus, Israel was in a double bind. The Gentile people of Nineveh repented whereas the people of Israel did not; and the prophet who had now come to Israel was a "greater than Jonah". If Gentiles repented at the proclamation of a lesser figure how great will Israel's condemnation be at her failure to respond to the greater, Jesus. Thus, Jesus remarked, "The men of Nineveh would rise at the judgement with this generation and condemn it" (Matthew 12:41).

Gentile cities of Tyre, Sidon and Sodom would fare better on the Day of Judgement than the northern Galilean towns of Chorazin, Bethsaida and Capernaum which had not repented despite the "mighty works" Jesus had done in them (Matthew 11:20-24).

The totality of Jesus' activity—present and future—was connected with Israel and the Nations. Jesus' death, of which he often spoke (cf. Mark 2:20), was brought about by *both* Israel and the Nations. Representatives of both groups— the chief priests representing Israel and Pilate representing the Gentiles—would share the responsibility for Jesus' death (Mark 10:33-34).

Yet, mysteriously, Jesus died for both groups; he died inclusively, for the redemption of "many" people—from both Israel and the Nations (Mark 10:45; 14:24). Israel would be judged according to her welcome given to the One who came announcing the Kingdom and calling for repentance. Likewise the Nations would be judged according to the welcome they will give to the "brothers" of the King, his apostles who come in his name to make disciples of the Nations (Matthew 25:40; 28:19-20).

Jesus announced that there would be a critical period of time between the judgement of Israel and the opportunity for the Nations. Jesus enigmatically spoke of "*three* days" or the "*third* day."

At the time Jesus expelled the traders from the temple he said, "Destroy this temple and in three days I will raise it up" (John 2:19; cf. Mark 14:58; Acts 6:14).

This statement is to be understood as Jesus' prophecy that the temple of Israel would be destroyed and rebuilt *in three days*. Jesus subsequently spoke at length about the destruction of the temple as he looked across the Kidron Valley from the Mount of Olives (Mark 13:2, 14-23). The temple, which symbolised Israel, would be destroyed and replaced by another, in which all men—Jews and Gentiles—could meet. According to John, he spoke of the temple of his body, which would be raised after three days (2:20-21) and become the means of incorporating Israel and the Nations in the one fellowship. Jesus' action in clearing the temple must be understood as signifying his intention to destroy the old and to rebuild the new.

On another occasion (Luke 13:31-35) Jesus spoke of his entire ministry as symbolised by "three days". He cast out demons today and tomorrow and on the *third* day "he was perfected". The parallel structure of that saying also speaks of the prophet being killed in Jerusalem on the *third* day and that this would be the time when Israel's house would be forsaken. Jesus' perfection and Israel's destruction would be complete on the *third* day.

When Jesus was asked for a "sign" he referred to Jonah's call to repentance. As Jonah spent "three days in the belly of a huge fish" so the Son of man would spend "three days and nights in the heart of the earth". The [Gentile] Ninevites, who repented at the preaching of Jonah will stand up at the judgement to condemn Israel for her failure to heed the call to repent by one who was greater than Jonah. Moreover, Jonah had been three days in the fish; but Jesus had been three days in the grave (Matthew 12:40-41).

These enigmatic "three days" sayings were spoken early in Jesus' ministry. When he travelled for the last time to Jerusalem he spoke repeatedly and explicitly of being killed at the hands of the chief priests and the Gentiles and rising again "after three" days. It is clear that these "three days" would be critical for the judgement of Israel and the salvation of the Nations.

There is one key statement made by Jesus which, more than any other, opens the door for our understanding of his mission. This is Jesus' "rock" saying. In response to Peter's confession that Jesus is the Christ, the Son of the Living God, Jesus said, "On this rock I will build my church, and the powers of death shall not prevail against it" (Matthew 16:18).

One thousand years earlier Nathan had prophesied to King David that God would establish a kingdom for his descendant, one who would "build a house" for Yahweh's name (2 Samuel 7:12-13). Jesus saw himself as that "son of David" who would build a "house" or "church" for the name of God, to be drawn from Israel and the Nations. Jesus would indeed destroy the temple. But there will be a new temple, which he will (begin to) build after "three days". The risen Jesus continues to build his church/house as his servants proclaim the gospel-message and men and women acknowledge that Jesus is the Christ of God, his Son.

What is the "rock" on which Jesus will build his church? Most probably Jesus is referring to Peter, spokesman of the Twelve, who has now declared Jesus to be the Christ, the Son of the Living God. These Twelve who confess Jesus to be Messiah are the foundation of the newly re-constituted covenant people of God.

Earlier Jesus taught a parable of a tiny seed that would become a giant tree, in which the birds of the air would find shelter (Mark 4:30-32). The idea of the great tree with sheltering birds, which appears in the prophets, is used by Jesus to portray the smallness of the Twelve at that time, in contrast with the greatness of his covenant people at the End. The Gentiles are represented in this parable by the image of the birds which shelter in the great tree (cf. Ezekiel 31:6,12).

Whether as a "rock" or a "seed" Jesus depicts his Twelve as the beginnings of a great covenantal community, called out of Israel, which would ultimately encompass the Nations in the End-time.

The mission and intention of Jesus, while deeply conscious of the message of the prophets of Israel, of whom he was self-consciously the last, goes back even further than David and Nathan's prophecy to him. Jesus' thinking went back to Abraham and God's promise to him. God assured Abraham that in his descendants all the families of the earth would be blessed (Genesis 12:3; 22:18). Jesus was that descendant of Abraham; he saw the blessing of the Nations flowing out from him.

As the son of Abraham and the son of David, Jesus fulfils the great purposes of God for Israel and the Nations, in fact for the whole of humanity. Recent New Quest scholarship in which Jesus is interpreted exclusively in Jewish categories, gives Jesus little, if any application beyond the Jewish people of the first century. But in his filial face, as revealed to the Twelve, Jesus is Lord of all peoples—Israel and the Nations.

While it has to be agreed with deep sorrow that Jewish people throughout history have suffered much at the hands of Christians, it must be pointed out that Jesus is not anti-semitic. Jesus' prophecy of the destruction of the temple and his promise to the Nations in no way precludes members of the people of Israel from accepting his person and message. Paul the apostle to the Gentiles envisaged a future ingathering of the people of Israel for her Messiah, Jesus (Romans 11:11ff). Jesus is God's gift to humanity expressed for the two great peoples which compose it—Jews and Gentiles. He loved, welcomed and died for both, for "many". No racial group can make any special claim on Jesus as being exclusively their possession, nor reject him as peculiarly abhorrent to them. Jesus the Jew is Lord of All.

Further reading:
P. Barnett, *Bethlehem to Patmos,* (Sydney, Hodder and Stoughton, 1989)
J. Jeremias, *Jesus' Promise to the Nations* (London, SCM, 1958)
——*New Testament Theology I* (London, SCM, 1971)
B. Meyer, *The Aims of Jesus* (London, SCM, 1979)
J.A.T. Robinson, *The Priority of John,* (London, SCM, 1985)
E. Stauffer, *Jesus and His Story,* (New York, Knopf, 1974)

8 THE IDENTITY OF JESUS

Jesus the Son of Man discloses his identity to the Twelve—as Son of God and as Servant of the Lord. Only the Jesus of two faces—in particular of the filial face—could have inspired early Christianity. The one-sided Jewish Jesus as proposed by some New Quest scholars could never have done so.

It is clear from the previous chapter that Jesus had a powerful sense of mission. Did he have an equally clear sense of his own identity? Can we identify Jesus' consciousness of himself? In this chapter we get to the matter; we see the filial face of Jesus.

The New Quest expresses greater confidence than Bultmann in discovering Jesus' sense of identity. True to their twin emphases—the historical recoverability of Jesus and his Jewishness—many New Quest scholars are prepared to say who Jesus thought he was, namely someone with the profile of a first century Jew. In his important study *Jesus the Jew*, Vermes concluded that Jesus was "one of the holy miracle workers of Galilee" (p.223). According to Vermes, Jesus was regarded in his own day as a prophet, but the early Christians soon dispensed with this title preferring others like Christ, Lord and Son of God.

In one sense Vermes is correct. In his *public* teaching in the synagogues and to the crowds Jesus taught about God, specifically that the kingdom of God is near (Mark 1:14-15). It is noteworthy that Jesus did not teach directly about himself in public. The public perception of Jesus may well have been as a rabbi and/or a prophet who taught about God and his kingdom (cf. Mark 8:28; John 3:2). Vermes sees this face of Jesus, the public face of Jesus, through the eyes of his Galilean contemporaries.

Nonetheless, Vermes does not sufficiently take into account Jesus' teaching about himself to the Twelve *in private*. While to the Twelve Jesus explained his parables, saying that to them was given the mystery of the kingdom of God, for the people in general he spoke only in parables which were not explained (Mark 4:11). Thus for Jews at large Jesus remained as mystifying a figure as the parables he taught. It was mainly to the Twelve that he taught about himself and this teaching became the basis of the New Testament understanding of Jesus' identity—as One who knew himself to be the Son of God. It was Jesus' awareness that he was the Son of God which survived in the understanding of the earliest believers, illuminated and enhanced as it was after the first Easter and Pentecost (cf. Romans 1:4).

Here many New Quest scholars raise a fundamental difficulty. They point out that Jewish belief in the unity of God as in the credo "Hear O Israel: the Lord our God, the Lord is one" (Deuteronomy 6:4) rules out the possiblity that a man could be God. Since Jesus was a Jew and shared this belief that "Yahweh is one", they argue he could not have regarded himself as a divine figure. They also remind us that "the son of God" in the Old Testament, the scriptures Jesus the Jew upheld, was not at all a deity figure, but referred to the reigning monarch of Israel (e.g. Psalm 2:7; 2 Samuel 7:14). By Jesus' times "Son of God" was a synonym for the Anointed One, the Messiah. This can be seen in the high priest's question to Jesus: "Are you the Christ, the Son of the Blessed?" (Mark 14:61).

Therefore, when the early church refers to Jesus as "the Son of God" in the sense of deity, it is claimed there is a departure from what Jesus the Jew could have meant. The early church, therefore, either misunderstood or distorted Jesus' idea of "the Son of God".

The problem with this line of argument is that it pre-emptively locks Jesus into the box of first century Jewish theology. It does not allow the evidence about Jesus from the New Testament to define his identity, but defines him in advance in such a way that he cannot be other than a devout rabbi or a prophet.

So who did Jesus say he was? Here we run into another problem. The standard books on christology discuss Jesus according to the titles he used of himself—titles like the Son of Man, the Son of David, the Son of God, and the Servant. While Jesus spoke of himself in those terms, the feeling we have is one of unreality. This Jesus is unimaginable; he is not one person but many.

When we turn to read the Gospels, however, we do not encounter an unfocused person with four titles. Rather we meet a person who consistently and frequently refers to himself as "the Son of Man". To be sure he speaks of himself in the other terms mentioned, but always from the clearly focused standpoint of "the Son of Man".

There are many different interpretations of the Son of Man from the one following—including that the term was a mere circumlocution for "I" and that the future Son of Man prophesied by Jesus was not Jesus himself. For a review and reply to these and other differing views see S. Kim, *The Son of Man as the Son of God* (pp.7–37).

THE SON OF MAN

What, then, does Jesus mean by "the Son of Man"? The position taken here on this hotly debated question is that Jesus' understanding on "the Son of Man" has been formed by the dream-vision of Daniel 7:1-14. We read there of a human figure ("one like a son of man") who comes into the presence of God ("the Ancient of Days") to receive everlasting and universal dominion over all nations. This son of man begins his sovereign power after the various beast-like empires have risen and fallen. By referring to himself as *the* "Son of Man" Jesus is saying he is *that* "son of man" prophesied by Daniel 7 (See Mark 8:38-9:1; 14:62).

The latter half of Daniel 7, however, gives the interpretation of the dream-vision. We are very surprised to read in these verses that the persecuted "saints of the Most High will receive the kingdom and will possess it forever" (7:18 cf. 7:27). "One like a son of man" is now referred to as "saints of the Most High". This is usually taken to mean that the "son of man" is the representative and head of "the saints of the Most High". As in the four kingdoms where the kings represent and rule over the kingdoms so the "son of man" represents and rules "the saints of the Most High". Together, he and they, will rule the Nations forever.

In our opinion Daniel 7 was extremely influential in the thinking of Jesus. If Jesus saw himself as that "Son of Man" then he called the Twelve to be the embryo of the "saints of the Most High". They are the tiny *seed* which will become the giant tree in which the birds (= the Nations) will find shelter (Mark 4:30–32). They who now confess him as the Christ, through their spokesman Peter, are the *rock* on which Jesus will build his community of the End-time (Matthew 16:18). They are his *little flock* who are not to be afraid; their Father will give them the kingdom (Luke 12:32).If the Twelve are seed, rock and flock, then Jesus is sower, builder and shepherd.

The Twelve and other faithful disciples with them form the nucleus of the people with whom God has now made a new covenant through the blood of the Son of Man (Luke 22:20). They, and those who become attached to them in the course of history, are the ones over whom God's kingdom rules within history and who will share that rule with the Son of Man at his second advent. On the eve of his death Jesus told the Twelve:

I confer on you a kingdom, just as my father conferred one on me, so that you may eat and drink at my table in my kingdom and sit on thrones, judging the twelve tribes of Israel (Luke 22:29–30; cf. 1 Corinthians 6:1–2).

The Son of Man emphasis in the teaching of Jesus is a good argument against confining Jesus within the limits of first century Judaism. Within Judaism of the period the Sabbath was sacrosanct. Yet Jesus, Jew though he undoubtedly was, deliberately broke the Sabbath declaring "The Son of Man is Lord even of the Sabbath" (Mark 2:28). Here is the Unshrunk Patch tearing the old coat of Judaism,

Jesus' New Wine destroying the wineskins of the Old Covenant.

According to Jesus, the Son of Man is characterised by God-given authority. He is the One delegated by God to perform important functions on behalf of God. In this regard Jesus twice uses the word *exousia*, "delegated authority", of the Son of Man. Thus Jesus as the Son of Man is God's human representative to man in the whole range of God's eschatological dealings with man, exercising forgiveness and judgement on God's behalf: "The Son of Man has authority on earth to forgive sins" (Mark 2:10); "The Father has given [the Son] authority to execute judgement, because he is the Son of Man" (John 5:27).

In Jesus' revelation of him the Son of Man is characterised by mystery and majesty. In the earlier part of his ministry when he publicly declared the critical nearness of the kingdom of God, Jesus referred in private to the mysterious, parable-like character of the Son of Man. In the latter part of Jesus' ministry, however, after his humiliation, the Son of Man will be characterised by majesty.

Thus it becomes clear that the kingdom of God, which Jesus said was near, actually comes—comes *in power*—with the humiliation followed by the vindication of the Son of Man at the first Easter.

THE SON OF MAN AS THE SON OF GOD

We now consider the first example of one of the "titles" of Jesus from the standpoint of the Son of Man. The focus is not divided between the Son of Man and the Son of God. Jesus as Son of God is a function of the eschatological judge-king, the Son of Man.

S. Kim (pp.1–6) points out that in each of the four Gospels Jesus speaks of God as the Father of the Son of Man (Mark 8:38; Matthew 25:34; Luke 22:54–71; John 5:26f). According to Kim the identification is the more likely to be authentic because it is indirect in each case. It is also "in agreement with the mysterious or puzzling nature of 'the Son of Man' on the lips of Jesus" (p.6).

But who is this Son of God? Are the New Quest scholars, and indeed many other scholars before them, correct in identifying this phrase as messianic and nothing more? In our opinion Jesus means much more than that.

First, we should notice that Jesus himself rarely uses the phrase "the Son of God". Others—the Evangelists as well as various people who met Jesus—refer to or address him as the Son of God. But it is not Jesus' practice to speak of himself in that way. Rather, he will speak of God as "my Father" or, in relationship to the Son of Man, "his Father". And he will describe himself as "the Son" or as "the beloved Son". This nuance emerges in the following well-known statement: "All things have been delivered to me by my Father; and no one knows the Son except the Father; and no one knows the Father except the Son" (Matthew 11:26–27/Luke 10:22). This is the language of personal relationship between Jesus and his Father.

Second, the survival in the Gospels of the Aramaic word *Abba* reinforces the personal, rather than the messianic nature of the sonship references. This domestic mode of address to God is without parallel in Jewish literature. According to J. Jeremias (p.73): "[Jesus] spoke with God like a child with his father: confidently and securely and at the same time with reverence and with readiness to obey." Here is the filial, rather than the messianic consciousness of Jesus.

Kim's comment (p.75) should be noted:

Both the *abba*-address and the self-designation "the Son of Man" are the most striking of the unique features of Jesus, and they express his self-understanding more clearly than anything else. Therefore they must have had a close material connection with each other.

Confirmation of this is to be found in the early Christians' address to God as "our Father" (1 Thessalonians 1:3). Indeed even the Gentile churches knew the word *abba*, Father (Romans 8:15; Galatians 4:6). If, to the Son of Man, God was *abba*, then he was also to be *abba* to the Twelve and to those who became historically attached to them in the new covenant people of God.

This *abba*-Son relationship, however, was not entered into

by the Jewish people of the day who saw and heard Jesus. Just as the meaning of the parables was not "given" to them (Mark 4:11), but only to the Twelve, so too the unique Father-Son relationship between Yahweh and Jesus was "hidden" from the people at large. Only the Father knows the Son; only the Son knows the Father. But the Son reveals the Father to those whom he chooses—namely the Twelve. (Matthew 11:25-27). Likewise the Father reveals the Son to the Twelve (Matthew 16:16-17).

The Nicodemus incident illustrates this. Nicodemus recognised Jesus as a "teacher. . .come from God" (John 3:2), that is, as a rabbi. According to Jesus, however, only by supernatural rebirth will it be possible for Israel, as represented by this distinguished representative (3:7), to enter the kingdom of God (3:3,5), that is to recognise Jesus, not as a mere rabbi, but as God's "one and only Son" (3:16).

Once again investigation of the evidence has proved effective against New Quest strictures which limit "the Son of God" to the messianic categories in first century Judaism. Jesus, Jew though he was, has broken out of such constraints. He has re-defined Son of God from a messianic to a filial meaning.

Did Jesus claim to be divine, to be "God"? The answer is "Yes", but he made the claim obliquely and indirectly.

There are two occasions when Jesus' words are to be interpreted as an oblique claim to deity.

On one occasion he declared the paralysed man's sins forgiven (Mark 2:5). The scribes who were present declared this to be a blasphemy for who could forgive sins but God alone (See, e.g. Psalm 130:4).

On another occasion he commanded the wealthy man to "follow me" as the way to eternal life. In the ensuing conversation Jesus taught that to follow him was, in effect, to keep the Ten Commandments, including the first which repudiates any god except Yahweh (Mark 10:21). Who but Yahweh present with his people could make such a demand?

Jesus regarded his words of teaching as eternal, as eternal as God's words. "Heaven and earth shall pass away, but my words shall not pass away," he said (Matthew 24:35). But Isaiah had written: ". . .the word of our God stands forever" (Isaiah 40:8).

Jesus also applied to himself descriptions which were used in the Old Testament of the God of Israel. Early in his ministry Jesus described himself as the bridegroom. "Can the wedding guests fast while the bridegroom is with them?" he asked (Mark 2:19). But the bridegoom was an image traditionally used for the God of Israel. "As a bridegroom rejoicing over the bride, your God will rejoice over you"(Isaiah 62:5).

Another descriptive role Jesus applied to himself was the shepherd. ". . .Strike the shepherd, and the sheep will be scattered", he said (Mark 14:27 cf. John 10:11-16). But the shepherd was a familiar description of Yahweh, Israel, Israel's God (e.g. Psalm 23:1; Ezekiel 34:15).

"Rock" was another title for Yahweh that Jesus applied to himself. The prophet Isaiah wrote: "Behold I am laying in Zion for a foundation, a stone, a tested stone." (Isaiah 28:16). Jesus taught that to build one's life on his teachings was to build on a rock (Matthew 7:24-27).

Most significantly of all, however, Jesus spoke of himself as I AM, the very words by which Yahweh disclosed his identity to Moses (Exodus 3:14). Thus when he walked on the water, he told the disciples "Be not afraid, *I am*" (my translation), a statement whose probable historicity is enhanced because it appears in two separate and independent sources (Mark 6:50; John 6:20).

Three times in John 8 Jesus refers to himself in that way: ". . .you will die in your sins, unless you believe I am. . ." (v.24); "When you have lifted up the Son of Man, then you will know that I am. . ." (v.28); ". . .before Abraham was, I am." (v.58).

When the soldiers and temple police approached Jesus in the garden beyond the Kidron Valley, he asked, "Whom do you seek?" whereupon they replied, "Jesus of Nazareth." At his answer, "*I am*", those who came to arrest him fell to the ground (John 18:5-6).

Clearly the fourth evangelist portrays Jesus declaring himself to be Yahweh among his people.

Further evidence is to be seen in Jesus' reply to the high priest's question: "Are you the Christ, the Son of the Blessed?" Jesus said: "I am and you shall see the Son of Man seated at the right hand of Power, and coming with the clouds of heaven." At this they accused him of blasphemy (Mark 14:62–63).

Finally, Jesus prophesied that: "Many will come in my name saying, 'I am' and they will lead many astray". These false prophets will say "I am", in imitation of Jesus. This suggests that Jesus did in fact use those words *I am* of himself, thereby claiming deity (Mark 13:6).

On the basis of this evidence it appears that Jesus claimed to be Yahweh present with his people, though in subtle and indirect ways. After the resurrection, however, Jesus' deity was confirmed and made explicit in the worship of the earliest Christian communities of Jesus as their *Lord*. To the original Aramaic-speaking church in Jerusalem Jesus was invoked as *Mara* and in the Greek churches as *Kyrios* (cf 1 Corinthians 16:22).

During his historic ministry the disciples had asked, "Who then is this, that even wind and sea obey him?" (Mark 4:41). After the resurrection his followers gave the answer: "Jesus is Lord".

THE SON OF MAN AS THE SERVANT OF THE LORD.

Again we encounter Jesus portraying himself in another persona, yet from the standpoint of the Son of Man: "For even the Son of Man came not to be served but to serve and to give his life a ransom for many" (Mark 10:45); "This is my blood of the covenant, which is poured out for many" (Mark 14:24).

We come now to a facet of Jesus' persona which is utterly paradoxical—that he was the Servant of God as prophesied by Isaiah. Isaiah wrote a number of poems about a humble servant of God, who would be gravely mistreated, and whose death would somehow save others from God's punishment. "My servant will justify many, as he will bear their iniquities. . . he bore the sin of many. . . " (Isaiah 53:11–12).

As the Son of Man, Jesus will atone for the sins of the "saints of the Most High"—for the Twelve and those who would be added to them—Jews and Gentiles as the re-constituted people of God. Kim comments:

His death atones for those who would be represented by him...and dedicates them to God as his new eschatological people. Therefore this death is a sacrifice that inaugurates a new covenant (p.73).

The earliest recorded preaching (Acts 3:13,16; 4:27,30; 8:32ff) and the letters of the New Testament declare that the death of Jesus was in fulfilment of Isaiah's prophecies about the Servant who died for many (cf Romans 4:25; 8:32,34; 1 Peter 2:21-15). This interpretation originated with Jesus himself, as reflected in the passages quoted above.

As the "Son of man" from Daniel 7 and as the "servant of the Lord" from Isaiah 53 Jesus thus fused within himself respectively, in O. Cullmann's words, "the highest conceivable declaration of exaltation" and "the expression of deepest humiliation" (*The Christology of the New Testament*, p.161).

An old, rarely used Greek word, *agape*, had to be infused with new meaning to portray the special quality of sacrificial love which characterised the life of the Son of Man on the one hand, and which would become the distinguishing mark of his people, on the other (John 13:34-35; Mark 10:41-45). This word *agape*, which occurs a mere handful of times prior to Jesus, is found hundreds of times within the New Testament as a noun and verb. In effect a new word came into use to denote the new quality of love embodied in the Son of Man and his covenant community.

That the Son of Man must suffer and give his life a ransom for many—both Jews and Gentiles—did not form part of mainstream thought of first century Judaism. "Christ crucified" was an offence to Jews—both in prospect and retrospect (Mark 8:32; 1 Corinthians 1:23). The Son of Man as a suffering Servant, as taught by Jesus the Jew, was peculiar to him. Once more we see Jesus to be different from, not typical of, the Judaism of the times.

THE SON OF MAN AS MESSIAH

According to the earliest traditions of the New Testament, Jesus "was descended from David according to the flesh" (Romans 1:3; cf 2 Timothy 2:8). This is widely reflected elsewhere in the New Testament—in the mission preaching of Peter and Paul in the Acts, in the opening sentence and in the genealogy of Matthew, in the genealogy of Luke and in the understanding of the Book of Revelation and the letter to the Hebrews.

There is little doubt that Jesus regarded himself as the royal son of David, the long-awaited Messiah of Israel. When Peter acknowledged that Jesus was the Christ, Jesus replied, "on this rock [Peter confessing Jesus to be the Christ] I will build my church" (Matthew 16:18).

Jesus consciously spoke these words to fulfil the prophecy of Nathan to David. Yahweh, speaking through Nathan to David, said, "[Your descendant] shall build a house for my name, and I will establish the throne of his kingdom forever" (2 Samuel 7:13).

Clearly Jesus saw himself as that *descendant* of David, who would sit on the throne of David for ever and who would "build a house" for the name of Yahweh. Accordingly Jesus pronounced the existing "house" of God to be doomed, and cleared the merchants from it as a sign that it was doomed, that it was soon to be replaced by another "house" (= his church) that he would raise up in the space of three days.

Although Jesus knew himself to be the Messiah, the King of Israel, he was not usually willing to accept the title from the Jews, though it was sometimes given (John 1:49; 4:26; Mark 8:29 cf. 14:61). Jesus' reluctance to accept any messianic recognition was on account of the Jews' contemporary desire for a triumphalist, military messiah who would come to deliver Israel from the Gentiles. Moreover, to have publicized this title in Galilee would have brought rapid execution from the incumbent tetrarch, Herod Antipas.

As in the other "titles" Jesus spoke from the standpoint of the Son of Man. While not denying that he was the Messiah he preferred to define his messiahship primarily in terms of his character as the Son of Man. His was to be a heavenly kingship, to be exercised over the new End-Time community composed of people from Israel and the Nations, a "house" which would be characterised by reconciliation and restoration.

Despite Jesus' silence on the matter of his messiahship, however, it was as Messiah that he was arrested, found guilty and executed; the Romans' *titulus* on his cross read "King of the Jews". He would be proclaimed as the Christ, surnamed as Christ and his people called "Christians".

JESUS AND MIRACLES

Jesus' words reveal him to have been the Son of Man who was also conscious of having been the Son of God and the Son of David.

As it happens, the miracles of Jesus are God's confirmation that Jesus' consciousness is true.

Jesus pointed to a miracle in regard to his consciousness and claim to be the Son of Man. He said to a paralysed man, whose sins he had declared forgiven, "Rise, take up your pallet and walk...that you may know that the Son of Man has authority on earth to forgive sins" (Mark 2:9–10).

The healing of the paralysed man, which then occurred, was a visible demonstration of Jesus' claim to be the Son of Man, authorised by God to forgive sins on earth. Human reasoning could not confirm the claim of the Son of Man to have authority to forgive sins; but the dramatic healing of an immobilized cripple visibly demonstrated the truth of Jesus' claim to forgive sins.

Likewise, Jesus appealed to his miracles (= his "works") when challenged about his claim to be the Son of God. He said to the Jews who sought to stone him:

Do you say of him whom the Father consecrated and sent into the world, "You are blaspheming," because I said "I am the Son of God"? If I am not doing the works of my Father, then do not believe me; but if I do them, even though you do not believe me,believe the works, that you may know and understand that the Father is in me and I am in the Father (John 10:36–38).

The works of Jesus establish his identity as the Son of the Father. His creation of water from wine, his multiplication of bread and fish for the multitude, his healing of the crippled and the blind, his gift of life to the dead Lazarus are all, properly speaking, the *works* of God the creator, which, however, Jesus has done, establishing his Son-to-Father relationship with God.

When John the Baptist enquired whether in fact Jesus was the long-awaited Christ (= Messiah), he told John's messengers to tell him what they had heard and seen, "the blind receive their sight and the lame walk, lepers are cleansed and the deaf hear, the dead are raised up and the poor have the good news preached to them" (Matthew 11:2–5).

Jesus pointed to his miracles of healing in answer to the question are you the Christ?

Jesus was conscious that as the Son of Man he was the Son of God and the Son of David. His miracles confirmed the reality of his claims.

JESUS: AN EMOTIONAL PERSONALITY

Although the gospel-writers focus the readers' attention on Jesus, he is quite unlike the heroic figures in the general literature of the period. Those figures tend to be impassive, emotionless. But Jesus emerges from the Gospels, especially the Gospel of Mark, as a vital and strongly emotional personality.

His own words disclose something of his perception of himself. He said, "I am meek and lowly of heart" (Matthew 11:29). He gently addressed Jairus' lifeless daughter in Aramaic "*talitha*...little lamb" (Mark 5:41). On the night of his arrest he prayed in Gethsemane, "My soul is very sorrowful, even to death" (Mark 14:34). From the cross he cried out to God in Aramaic, "*Eloi, Eloi, lama sabachthani*...my God, my God, why have you forsaken me?" (Mark 15:34). Jesus' utterances reveal him to have had identifiable human emotions and reactions.

The disciples' perception of Jesus' character is also discernible, particularly in the Gospel of Mark. Love and compassion are attributed to him (10:21; 1:41; 6:34; 8:2). But so, too, is sternness (1:42) and anger (3:5) which provoked him to "look around" at people in a manner that was vividly recollected (3:5,34; 5:32; 10:23; 11:11). He "threw out" various people...a leper whom he had healed, from his presence (1:43); mourners from the house of Jairus (5:40); traders from the Temple (11:15). He "rebuked" demons (1:25; 9:25) and a raging wind (4:39) calling upon them to "be silent", and also Peter with the words, "Get behind me Satan" (8:33). Yet his disciples also perceived him to have been profoundly distressed at Gethsemane on the eve of his crucifixion (14:33).

Jesus' personal impact on his circle of followers has left its mark in the gospel records. Stanton commented that in the Gospels may be seen "a rich and full portrait [of Jesus]." (p.171)

JESUS' IDENTITY

Jesus must have made an exceptional impact on his followers; the movement established by him continued after his death. Other Jewish movements of the time died with the death of their leaders.

Jesus' followers, however, did not disband when he was no longer physically present with them. In fact, the two or three year period after the death of Jesus was one of intense activity in the earliest community of believers.

A twelfth member, Matthias, was elected to the college of apostles, to replace Judas the betrayer. The original followers of Jesus clearly understood that it was their master's will that the new messianic community was to be founded on twelve men.

Many of the sayings of Jesus were gathered together and committed either to memory or to writing at that time. A narrative of the events of Jesus' last days leading up to and including his death and resurrection was written.

The Old Testament was carefully read, to see how its prophecies had been fulfilled in Jesus. A list of Old Testament prophecies which were seen to have been fulfilled in Jesus was compiled. Quotations from these recognised prophecies occur frequently within the New Testament.

An outline statement of the gospel-message about Christ—his death for our sins, his burial, his resurrection on the third day, his appearances in chronological order to various people—was formulated. A liturgical summary for use at the Lord's Supper, based on the events at the Last Supper on the night of his betrayal, was drawn up. Both the gospel-outline and the Lord's Supper traditions, as formulated at this time, are reproduced intact in Paul's first letter to the Corinthians. As we point out in chapter 10, these traditions were "delivered" to Paul within four years of the death and resurrection of Jesus.

It is clear, therefore, that the first two or three years of the earliest community of believers in Jerusalem was a period of significant theological reflection. But this only occurred because of the great impact of Jesus upon his first followers.

Logically speaking, only an exceptional person could have made the impact Jesus made upon the movement which arose immediately after his death. Above all, however, his resurrection from the dead is the only satisfactory explanation for the remarkable level of activity focused on Jesus which occurred at that time.

This practical observation is not always apparent in the profiles of Jesus which scholars have attempted to reconstruct. It is very unlikely, for example, that Vermes' devout rabbi, or Sanders' eschatological prophet could have set early Christianity in motion. The various portrayals of Jesus produced by these scholars and by the liberal protestant scholars before them are so pale and unremarkable as to have disappeared without leaving much of a mark in history. Such Jesuses would never have launched early Christianity.

Further Reading:

P.W. Barnett, *Bethlehem to Patmos*, (Sydney, Hodder and Stoughton, 1989)

C. Caragounis, *The Son of Man*, (Tübingen, Mohr, 1986)

O. Cullmann, *The Christology of the New Testament*, (London, SCM, 1959)

R.T. France, *Jesus and the Old Testament*, (London, Tyndale, 1971)

M. Hengel, *The Son of God*, (London, SCM, 1975)
——*The Atonement*, (London, SCM, 1981)
——*Between Jesus and Paul*, (London, SCM, 1983)
J. Jeremias, *The Theology of the New Testament* 1, (London, SCM, 1971)
S. Kim, *The Son of Man as the Son of God,* (Tübingen, Mohr/Grand Rapids, Eerdmans, 1985)
G.E. Ladd, *The Presence of the Future*, (Grand Rapids, Eerdmans, 1974)
E. Lemcio, "The Intention of the Evangelist, Mark", *New Testament Studies* 32/2, 1986, pp.187-206
R.N. Longenecker, *The Christology of Early Jewish Christianity*, (Grand Rapids, Baker, 1981)
I.H. Marshall, *The Origins of New Testament Christology*, (Leicester, IVP, 1977)
C.F.D. Moule, *The Origin of Christology,* (Cambridge, Cambridge University Press, 1978)
G.N. Stanton, *Jesus of Nazareth in New Testament Preaching*, (London, CUP, 1974)
W. Zimmerli and J. Jeremias, *The Servant of God*, (London, SCM, 1957).

9 BETWEEN JESUS AND PAUL

Those who claim that Jesus' only face was that of a rabbi or prophet are forced to explain the exalted view of Jesus reflected in the literature of early Christianity. The usual explanation is that Paul invented Christianity. But Paul's letters are very early and the teaching contained in them goes back almost to the time of Jesus himself.

In the controversial film *The Last Temptation of Christ* based on Nikos Kazantzakis' novel, there is a fantasy scene in which Jesus imagines hearing what would be the later gospel-preaching of the apostle Paul, (whom the film regards as the true founder of Christianity). Jesus rebukes Paul for preaching the crucified and risen saviour saying, "I'm a man like everyone else. Why are you spreading these lies?" Paul replies, "I'm glad I met you. Now I'm rid of you... I've created truth out of longing and faith... If it's necessary to save the world to crucify you, then I'll crucify you—and I'll resurrect you, like it or not. The enemy is death and I'll defeat death by resurrecting you—Jesus of Nazareth, Son of God, Messiah."

The film expresses what many people feel, both scholars and ordinary people, that the apostle Paul has made Jesus into someone else. This is implicit in the writings of those New Quest authors who believe Jesus to be no more than a rabbi or a prophet. The position taken here, however, is that Paul and other New Testament letter-writers have accurately transmitted Jesus' own view of himself.

The traditional liberal position has been that Paul was responsible for changing Jesus. It is also to be found in many New Quest writers. Hyam Maccoby, for example, who regards Jesus as a Pharisee attributes "the invention of Christianity" to Paul, whom he dubs "the myth maker". To reach these conclusions it is necessary for Maccoby to take the extreme view that Paul was not a Pharisee, in fact not even a Jew! Maccoby's understanding of Jesus and Paul is drawn from the writings of the Ebionites, Jewish Christians of later centuries who held very weak views about Jesus; the evidence from the New Testament, the literature reflecting Jesus' impact on the Twelve, is largely disregarded.

So, did Paul invent Christianity?

The rock on which all these and other "low" views of Jesus stumble—that he was only a rabbi or prophet—is the brevity of time which separates Jesus the historical figure from the first written evidence about him, namely the letters of Paul.

We know the time span in which Paul's letters were written. Galatians may have been written as early as 49—the scholars are divided. Some say the mid fifties. First and Second Thessalonians, however, were certainly written in 50/51. First and Second Corinthians, along with Romans, were completed by 57. Six of Paul's letters, including his longest and most important, may be securely dated between 49 or 50 and 57.

The first Easter, according to experts in ancient date fixing, must have occurred either in 30 or 33. (This book, following H. Hoehner, opts for 33). This means that only seventeen years elapsed between Jesus and the earliest of Paul's letters. Paul's letters, however, reflect that, by the time they were written, Jesus was regarded as an exalted and divine figure—as the Christ, the Lord, and the Son of God. There is not the slightest trace of evidence that Jesus is thought of only as a rabbi or prophet. If Jesus of Nazareth was, in reality, one of those lowly figures, he has been exalted in an astonishingly brief period.

But there is more to be said.

First, the beliefs about Jesus which Paul expresses in his letters when they first appear in the early fifties could not have been new to him at the time of writing. His view of Jesus as an exalted figure was significantly formed at the time of writing and must pre-date his letters by at least some years.

Second, Paul quotes certain statements about Jesus in his letters which, as he himself tells us, he did not compose; he "received" these statements from others who were believers before him. In 1 Corinthians, Paul quotes two of these "received" statements, concerning:

the Last Supper	(1 Corinthians 11:23–26)
and	
the Gospel Outline	(1 Corinthians 15:3–8)

When and from whom did Paul "receive" these traditions?

The most probable time was the occasion of Paul's first visit to Jerusalem after his "call" on the road to Damascus; the most likely "deliverers" of these traditions were Cephas (=Peter) and James. Cephas and James were the only two apostles Paul "saw" on that occasion in Jerusalem (Galatians 1:18–19). Moreover, Cephas and James are the only two apostles actually named in the list of those to whom the risen Lord appeared in the statement of the gospel outline in 1 Corinthians 15:3–8. Cephas and/or James are the most likely formulators of the tradition that the Risen Jesus appeared on those five separate occasions. Therefore it was probably Cephas (and/or James) who "delivered" to Paul the tradition about the death and resurrection of Christ.

1 Corinthians 15:5,7:	Galatians 1:18–19:
	After three years I
[Christ] appeared to	went up to Jerusalem
Cephas...	to visit *Cephas*,
	...But I saw none of
Then he appeared to	the other apostles
James	except *James* the
	Lord's brother.

There are other possible occasions when Paul may have "received" this information—from Ananias in Damascus in c.34, from Barnabas in Antioch in c.45, from James, Cephas and John in Jerusalem in c.47 (Acts 9:10-19; 11:25-26; Galatians 2:1-9). The first option is too early for the traditions to have reached Damascus. The other options are too late since by then Paul had been "preaching the faith" and founding churches in Cilicia and Syria for about ten years—with doctrines acceptable to the Judaean churches (Galatians 1:21-24; cf Acts 15:41). It is more likely that Paul's first visit to Jerusalem after his conversion, in c.36, was the occasion when these traditions were "delivered" to him.

The formats of the traditions about the Lord's Supper and the gospel which Paul "received" are so similar as to suggest they were "delivered" to Paul from the one source—Cephas (and/or James).

The Last Supper:	The Gospel Outline:
For I *received* from the Lord what I *delivered* to you, *that* the Lord Jesus on the night he was betrayed.	For I *delivered* to you... what I also *received*, *that* Christ died for our sins... *that* he was buried...

The similarity of the formulae—I *received*, I *delivered*, *that*—suggests that both traditions were "received" at the same time from the same person or people.

The "calling" of Saul of Tarsus occurred about two years after the first Easter, that is in 34. Therefore Paul is a very early convert to the new movement; the time gap between the crucifixion and Paul's conversion is extremely brief. Three years later, in c.36, Paul the Christian returned to Jerusalem. (See Galatians 1:18 noting that part years were then counted as full years.) Between the time of the first Easter in 33 and Paul's return to Jerusalem in c.36 the traditions about the Last Supper/Lord's Supper and the gospel outline had been formulated, ready to "deliver".

The following time scale dramatically depicts the brevity of the period—and its closeness to Jesus—in which these traditions about him were formulated:

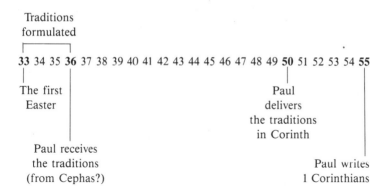

Traditions
formulated

33 34 35 **36** 37 38 39 40 41 42 43 44 45 46 47 48 49 **50** 51 52 53 54 **55**

The first   Paul
Easter   delivers
                                            the traditions
                                              in Corinth

   Paul receives
   the traditions
   (from Cephas?)   Paul writes
                                            1 Corinthians

In other words, many of the beliefs about Jesus which
are reflected in Paul's letters written in the early fifties—
that he was the Lord, that he was the Christ who died for
the sins of his people, that he was seen alive from the dead
on numerous occasions by some hundreds of people—are
quotations of traditions which were formulated no later than
three or four years after Jesus. What Vermes and Sanders
are not able to explain satisfactorily is how a Jesus executed
in so relatively lowly and unexceptional a role as a rabbi or
prophet could come to be regarded as "Lord" and "Christ"
within such a short period.

Moreover, we have to consider the case of Paul, himself,
a leading younger scribe of the sect of the Pharisees
(Galatians 1:13-14). How do we explain why he would be
prepared to devote his life to promoting the view that Jesus
was an exalted figure—the Christ, the Son of God and the
Lord—if he had been in reality a mere rabbi or prophet.
Paul's letters reveal him to have been a highly intelligent and
astute man, who is scarcely likely to have thrown away his
promising career as a scribe for the sake of a crucified rabbi
or prophet.

Since we know that Paul was in possession of many of
Jesus' teachings, we must assume that he checked the details
about Jesus' life and character and his resurrection with great
care before embarking on a long and exhausting career in
which he would suffer great privations and hardships. Let
any visitor to Israel, Greece or Turkey in the heat of high
summer reflect upon the great, danger-laden distances

travelled by Paul preaching from town to town and supporting himself by manual labour. Why would any up and coming scholar and teacher abandon his future and undergo a life of extreme difficulty and weariness for the cause of a crucified man, unless he was convinced that that man in his historic existence was one and the same person who confronted him as the heavenly Lord near Damascus?

It is my contention that it is much more likely that Jesus was conscious of being, and had claimed to be, not at all a rabbi or prophet but the Son of Man who was the Son of God and the Servant and that his resurrection confirmed to the Twelve and other close followers the rightness of his consciousness and his claims.

Further reading:
J. Finegan, *Handbook of Biblical Chronology*, (Princeton, Princeton University Press, 1964)

A.M. Hunter, *Paul and his Predecessors*, (London, SCM, 1961)

M. Hengel, *Acts and the History of Earliest Christianity*, (London, SCM, 1979)

H.W. Hoehner, *Chronological Aspects of the Life of Christ*, (Grand Rapids, Zondervan, 1977)

S. Kim, *The Origin of Paul's Gospel*, (Grand Rapids, Eerdmans, 1982)

10 THE MESSAGE AND THE MAN

The movement spread rapidly in the absence of its founder by means of a fourfold message about him. This fourfold message, however, is also central in the teaching of Jesus. There is no discontinuity: the message of Jesus becomes the message of early Christianity.

Jesus was crucified in 33, leaving behind a hundred or so Galilean supporters in Jerusalem. Yet within thirty years this movement had become big enough to be used as a scapegoat by the emperor Nero—to divert attention from himself—in the aftermath of the fire of Rome AD 64.

Historically speaking how did this movement spread without the physical presence of its founder? Clearly there must have been some verbal statement about Jesus which, in his absence became the instrument of the movement's growth?

We look in the first instance at the letters of Paul which were written between c.49–65. Less than twenty years separate Jesus from the earliest letters of Paul which provide early, first hand information about the beliefs and practices of the movement. They provide valuable information about the "message" of Christianity.

From these letters we discover that people first joined the movement through hearing a message about Jesus, which was called "the gospel" or "the word of God" (1 Thessalonians 2:8,13). Christianity, therefore, was a movement based on verbal communication, a message with carefully defined content.

Equally secure is the fact that, as we have already stated, Paul did not invent the message. Christians before Paul formulated the outline of that message and he "received" it from them. Paul merely "delivered" to others what he himself had previously "received". Paul here depicts himself as a young rabbi who has "delivered" to a pupil the "tradition" which he, Paul, had previously "received" from his teacher. The teacher of Paul was, as we have already said, Peter (and James?), whom Paul visited in Jerusalem within three years of his conversion (Galatians 1:18); Paul's "pupils" were the churches in Cilicia, Galatia, Macedonia, Achaia and Asia which he established.

Paul sets out that message in the course of his first letter to the Corinthians where he reminds the readers of what he first told them in Corinth in 50, "the gospel...which *you* received...what I received *I* delivered to you" (15:1,3).

Paul then tells the Corinthians precisely what it was he (in c.36) and they (in 50) in turn had "received":

> *that* Christ died for our sins in accordance with the scriptures
> *that* [Christ] was buried
> *that* [Christ] was raised on the third day in accordance with the scriptures
> *that* [Christ] appeared to Cephas

then		to the twelve
then	he appeared	to more than 500 brothers at one time...
then	he appeared	to James
then		to all the apostles.
last of all	he appeared also	to me...

This careful statement has all the marks of an oft-repeated creed or confession. The following points should be noted:

1 The fourfold *that* points to four statements about Christ which (Cephas?) *delivered* to Paul in c 36 which in turn Paul delivered to the Corinthians in 50 who *received* it.

2 The list of people to whom the risen Christ appeared, first to Cephas, to those mentioned each prefixed by "then" and "last of all" to Paul, suggests a precise chronological sequence of sightings.

Let it be repeated: Paul did not devise this information

about Christ. The form of words which appears in I Corinthians 15 predates the letter in which it is quoted by about twenty years, and goes back almost to the time of Jesus himself.

It was by "receiving" this verbally communicated message about Christ, his death, burial, resurrection and appearances, that the Christian movement spread to Corinth and, indeed, to all other places where churches sprang up.

As mentioned in a previous chapter these words confirm that the Christian movement had only one interest, its founder, Christ. He is central to every "that" in the gospel outline.

This puts it a little too baldly, however. Christ is no parachutist who just dropped from the sky into history, unheralded, only to disappear as mysteriously as he came. There is a fourfold structure of thought about Christ discernible in the gospel-message presented in the letters of Paul and others, which bears an important similarity to aspects of the teaching of Jesus recorded in the Gospels.

First, 1 Corinthians 15 indicates that Christ's death and resurrection were pre-figured in the Old Testament. These events focused on Jesus were "in accordance to the scriptures".

Second, Christ is not an isolated, enigmatic loner. Nor is he merely a man. Jesus is a supernatural being—the Son of God, no less. God is his Father. A filial-paternal relationship exists between Christ and God, such as can be true of no other man.

As it happens, Paul's second letter to the Corinthians also reminds the Corinthians of the message he had spoken to them when he first came to Corinth. "For the Son of God, Jesus Christ, whom we preached among you, Silvanus, Timothy and I... All the promises of God find their 'Yes' in him" (1:19–20; Acts 18:5).

This valuable reminiscence of Paul's mission preaching in the southern Greek metropolis in 50, sets Jesus in a twofold relationship with God. He is related to God as Son to Father and, as we have noticed in I Corinthians 15, his coming is the fulfilment of the promises made by God in the Old Testament scriptures.

Third, the message made the remarkable announcement that Christ had, in his coming, death and resurrection, inaugurated the last days. Paul wrote to the Galatians that: "When the time had fully come, God sent forth his Son...to redeem... God sent forth the Spirit of his Son" (4:4–6). According to Paul, Christ's people were those "upon whom the end of the ages has come" (1 Corinthians 10:11).

Christ had bisected history. Everything is different *now* (Greek: *nun*) a word Paul repeatedly uses, as for example: "Behold, now is the acceptable time; behold, now is the day of salvation" (2 Corinthians 6:2); and "We are now justified by (Christ's) blood... Christ, through whom we have now received our reconciliation... There is now no condemnation for those...in Christ Jesus..." (Romans 5:9,11; 8:1).

Paul is not alone among the letter-writers of the New Testament in seeing Christ as ending the old and inaugurating the final epoch. The letter to the Hebrews refers to "these *last* days" which began when God "spoke" finally in his Son's coming (1:1–2). The first letter of Peter declares that Christ was "made manifest at the end of the times" (1:20).

The letter-writers emphasise that Christ's actions are therefore final, absolute and irrepeatable. Paul, the writer to the Hebrews, Peter and Jude all employ the single word *hapax* to declare to their readers that Christ has acted for humanity "once and for all". The writer to the Hebrews, for example, states that "[Christ] appeared once for all at the end of the age to put away sin" (9:26; Romans 6:10; 1 Peter 3:18; Jude 5). Christ's coming, death and resurrection mark the beginning of the end-times, the last days.

Fourth, the gospel-message as embedded in the letters of Paul and others, declared that the risen Christ will return. Paul wrote from Corinth in 50 to the church in Thessalonica, which he had established the previous year, reminding them of their response to the word of the Lord:

> You turned to God from idols, to serve a living and true God, and to wait for his Son from heaven, whom he raised from the dead, Jesus, who delivers us from the wrath to come (1 Thessalonians 1:9–10).

Other letter-writers—the writer to the Hebrews, Peter, and John—emphasise the return of Jesus Christ (Hebrews 9:27–28; 1 Peter 1:7; 1 John 3:2).

By what "message" did this movement grow? Churches were established by means of a fourfold statement which focused on one person—Jesus Christ. According to snippets from the letters, the gospel-message announced that:

1 The prophecies of the Old Testament were fulfilled (in the death and resurrection of Christ).

2 The last Age has been inaugurated by him.

3 As the Christ and the Son of God, Jesus was a unique person.

4 Jesus will return.

We will now argue from the Gospels that these four things are also central in the teaching of Jesus. In other words, we affirm that the teachings Paul transmitted to the churches had their origin in the teaching of Jesus. Paul transmitted the teachings of Jesus, which had been handed to him. Jesus taught:

1 That the prophecies of the Old Testament are fulfilled: "I have come...to fulfil [law and prophets]" (Matthew 5:17).

2 That the New Age has come: "The time is fulfilled, and the kingdom of God is at hand" (Mark 1:15).

The first and second elements, those of Old Testament fulfilment and the inbreaking of the new age (the kingdom of God), are implicit in this single utterance of Jesus, made at the commencement of his public ministry in Galilee, "The time has come. The kingdom of God is near. Repent."

The kingdom of God was at hand because the time was fulfilled; the time was fulfilled because in Jesus the Law and the Prophets were fulfilled.

3 Jesus is the Son of God: "All things have been delivered to me by my Father; and no one knows the Son except the Father..." (Matthew 11:27/Luke 10:22).

In his allegory of the vineyard Jesus spoke of the various servants the owner sent to the vineyard—a clear reference to the various prophets sent by God to Israel. But *finally* (Greek: *eschaton*) God sent his beloved *Son* (Mark 12:2-7). Finality (i.e. fulfilment) and sonship are inseparable in the teaching of Jesus.

4 Jesus will return: "Then they will see the Son of Man coming in clouds with great power and glory..." (Mark 13:26).

The second coming of Jesus, which is so prominent in the letters of the New Testament, including the very early letters to the Thessalonians, is clearly embedded in the parables and sayings of Jesus (See e.g. Mark 13:34; Matthew 24:45–25:46; Luke 12:35–48; 18:1–8; 19:11–26).

Enough has been written above to establish that the fourfold structure of the gospel-message embedded in the letters of Paul and other writers is also found in the sayings of Jesus within the gospel traditions.

The view is sometimes put that Paul does not appear to say very much about the historic Jesus. It is assumed that a lengthy period of time separated Paul from the historical Jesus. As we have seen, however, the conversion of Saul of Tarsus occurred only about two years after the first Easter.

Paul was not cut off from information about Jesus, as is often assumed. The persecutor Saul had heard the teachings of the Hellenist Christian, Stephen. He had also heard the testimony of those believers whom he had executed (Acts 6:8–10; 7:54–8:1; 26:9–11). It is probable that Paul owed to Stephen much of what would be his later understanding about the way in which the new covenant had annulled the old (cf 2 Corinthians 3). The converted Paul stayed with Cephas for fifteen days and also saw James the Lord's brother (Galatians 1:18–19). Through Cephas and James the early life of Jesus, as well as his teachings and deeds in his public ministry, were available to Paul almost from the beginning of his time as a Christian.

It is no surprise, therefore, to know that Paul's letters are permeated with information about Jesus, as the following examples indicate:

1 There are allusions to the *teaching* of Jesus, for example, the duty to pay taxes (Romans 13:7/Mark 12:17)

2 The members of the movement to whom Paul wrote are repeatedly called upon to live like the *known character* of Jesus, for example his humility (Philippians 2:5/ Matthew 11:29)

3 Paul is aware of the sequence and nature of the *life* of Jesus:

a) his incarnation and birth (2 Corinthians 8:9)

b) his upbringing "under the Law" (Galatians 4:4-6)

c) the name of a brother—James (Galatians 1:19) and that there were other brothers (1 Corinthians 9:5)

d) his own distinctive teaching ("the Law of Christ"— e.g. Galatians 6:2)

e) his Last Supper on the night of his arrest and his betrayal (1 Corinthians 11:23)

f) his death by crucifixion, his burial, his resurrection on the third day and the chronological sequence of numerous appearances to many disciples (e.g. 1 Corinthians 15:3-5).

In fact, Paul had extensive knowledge of both Jesus' message and Jesus' character. It may be assumed that the churches established by Paul were given this information as part of the apostle's initial preaching and teaching to them (1 Thessalonians 2:14; 4:15; 2 Thessalonians 2:2,15; 3:6). Paul only refers to this Jesus-data to reinforce or to correct the churches' behaviour or understanding. Paul does not supply information about Jesus that his readers do not already know.

If we again ask where Paul obtained this information about Jesus the answer can only be: from those who were believers before him. Directly, or indirectly, therefore, Paul derived his data about Jesus from the Twelve. The Twelve in turn learned about Jesus from Jesus. He called them to come to him that they might learn from him (Matthew 11:28-29). He beckoned them from among their fellows to belong to his intimate circle. In their closeness to him they saw both sides of him—his face as rabbi and prophet, but above all his filial face.

Paul, therefore, is not the originator of traditions about Jesus, but their transmitter, in the following sequence:

JESUS $\rightarrow$ TWELVE $\rightarrow$ PAUL $\rightarrow$ GENTILE CHURCHES

This is not to deny the revelation the Son of God made to Paul en route to Damascus by which he became convinced that Jesus was the glorified Lord. Nonetheless it is clear that he was dependent on those who were believers before him for historical information about Jesus.

Our line of argument to date is historical in character and, we think, logical and reasonable. The letters of Paul, which are indisputably close in time to Jesus, reveal that the movement was spread by means of the gospel-message. These letters give snippets of the mission preaching of Paul, much of which was formulated by others very close to the time of Jesus. Based on these echoes of the message in the letters of Paul we are able to locate four major elements in the structure of that message by which the movement spread. We have now argued that those four elements were fundamental to the message of Jesus himself.

There is no gulf between the message of the man and the message about the man. Paul was not a mythmaker, but a faithful interpreter of the teachings of Jesus which had been "delivered" to him.

Further reading:

A.M. Hunter, *Paul and His Predecessors*, (London, SCM, 1961)

M. Hengel, *Acts and the History of Earliest Christianity,* (London, SCM, 1979)

H.W. Hoehner, *Chronological Aspects of the Life of Christ*, (Grand Rapids, Zondervan, 1977)

S. Kim, *The Origin of Paul's Gospel*, (Grand Rapids, Eerdmans, 1982)

H. Maccoby, *The Mythmaker: Paul and the Invention of Christianity,* (London, Weidenfeld and Nicholson, 1986)

11 THE EXALTED ONE IN THE TEACHING OF PAUL

The titles of exaltation of Jesus which appear in the letters of Paul are in each case earlier than his letters and go back towards the time of Jesus. Jesus himself is the impulse for these ways of thinking about him, transmitted by him, through the Twelve, to Paul and ultimately to the churches he established.

The letters of Paul—which begin to be written by 50, or even a year or two earlier—tell us who Paul thought Jesus was at that time, as his contemporary, so to speak. From these letters, however, we also discover who others thought Jesus was during that twenty year interval. This is because oral traditions about Jesus arose in the first two or three years after the resurrection and were kept alive in the creeds, confessions and worship of the early churches which are quoted and referred to in Paul's letters.

So, who was Jesus thought to be by the year 50, as reflected in Paul's letters?

Jesus was thought of in three ways, in particular: as Christ, the Son of God and the Lord.

CHRIST

Paul usually writes of *Jesus* Christ, as if Christ was a surname. "Christ", which is Greek for the Hebrew word

"Messiah", would not have meant very much to Gentiles of the time. This explains how the title Christ came to be used as Jesus' surname when Gentiles are being addressed (as they mostly are in Paul's letters).

Nonetheless, there are a number of references to Christ (without Jesus) in Paul's letters. These mostly refer to him as *the* Christ = the Messiah. This is Jesus' title, not his name, and it reflects a widespread early belief that Jesus was *the* Messiah/Christ.

These occurrences may be grouped in four ways:

1 Christ, the sender of "apostles"
Paul and his companions are "apostles of Christ" (1 Thessalonians 2:6) as presumably also were those whom Paul speaks of as "those who were apostles before me" (Galatians 1:17,19), in the two years between the resurrection of Jesus and the conversion of Paul. There were "apostles of Christ" from the time of the first Easter, indeed from the time of the mission of the Twelve (Mark 3:14; 6:30).

Paul wrote, in simple terms, "Christ... sent ["apostled"- Greek: *apesteilen*] me..." (1 Corinthians 1:17). In the original Hebraic terms Paul and the Twelve were the apostles of the Messiah, God's anointed king.

Since an apostle represents someone greater than himself, it is to be inferred that Christ, whom Paul and others represent, is a very great person. This is confirmed by the statement: "The head of every man is Christ" (1 Corinthians 11:3)

2 Christ, the crucified one
Paul makes constant reference to the scandalous death of Jesus by crucifixion. He told the Corinthians "I decided to know nothing among you except Jesus Christ and him crucified..." (1 Corinthians 2:2; cf. Galatians 3:1). Crucifixion was the Romans' way of suppressing the lower orders and humiliating self-styled kings. For their part Jews regarded a crucified person as "hanging on a tree", which according to Deuteronomy 21:23 meant he was under the curse of God. Paul's reason for persecuting believers had been that their leader finished up on a Roman cross, and there -

fore was automatically to be regarded as under the curse of
God. Paul had regarded Jesus of Nazareth as one who had
found his just deserts as a heretic and false-messiah who had
established a dangerous sect.

Jews at that time were expecting the coming of one whom
they called "the Christ" (Romans 9:5; Mark 12:35), who,
however, was envisaged as a triumphant national deliverer.
A crucified Messiah/Christ was a mockery, a contradiction
in terms, to Jews. It was from bitter experience of frequent
rejection by his people that Paul wrote: "We preach Christ
crucified, a stumbling block to Jews..." (1 Corinthians 1:23).

Here is the offensive paradox of the crucified Messiah
which runs like a scarlet thread throughout the New
Testament. It occurs first at Caesarea Philippi when Peter
confessed Jesus to be the Christ, whereupon Jesus spoke
immediately of his sufferings and death (Mark 8:31). The
same cruel irony is portrayed in the crucifixion scene where
the Romans' *titulus* "king (= Messiah) of the Jews" was
nailed above a *crucified* man (Mark 15:26,32). In the Book
of Revelation the angel calls out in a loud voice, for all
creation to hear, for someone worthy to open the scroll of
destiny to step forward. An elder declared that one was
worthy: "The Lion of the Tribe of Judah, the root of David",
the Messiah of Israel. But when John looked he saw not a
Lion but a Lamb, a Lamb moreover with a death wound!
Thus the aweful paradox of the Messiah *crucified* is stated
by John also, but in his characteristically symbolic terms
(Revelation 5:5-6).

3 The gospel of Christ

Paul often wrote of the "gospel of Christ" and the "word
of Christ" (e.g. 1 Thessalonians 3:2; Galatians 1:7; Romans
10:17), declaring also that "Christ is preached..." (1 Corinthians 15:12). From the many echoes of this preaching of
Christ in Paul's letters we know the outline of what was said,
an outline which preceded the writing of Paul's letters by
many years, going back (almost) to the time of Jesus.

Thus we may say that apostles of Christ preached the word
of Christ.

This Gospel of Christ Outline surfaces in a number of

places within the letters of Paul but never more clearly than in "received" material quoted by him in 1 Corinthians 15:3-5:

Christ died for our sins in accordance with the scriptures...

he was buried...

he was raised on the third day in accordance with the scriptures...

he appeared to Cephas...the twelve...more than five hundred...etc.

The twin pillars of this gospel are that the Messiah/Christ died (the truth of which is confirmed by the words "he was buried") *and* that the Messiah was raised on the third day (the truth of which is established by the words "he appeared to" certain named persons most of whom are still alive to verify the fact). Clearly we are meant to understand that the death and resurrection of the Messiah are genuine historical events.

These two pillars—the death and resurrection of the Messiah/Christ—are in fulfilment of the scriptures, as the New Testament often states (e.g. Luke 24:45-46; Acts 17:2-3). The death of the Messiah/Christ for "our sins" refers to Isaiah's prophecy about the Servant of the Lord who would be killed on account of "our sins" (Isaiah 53:5).

Paul constantly referred to the Messiah's atoning death, as for example in the passage following. This may have been Paul's most characteristic way of expressing the traditional teaching about the death of the Messiah in his own words: "In Christ God was reconciling the world to himself, not counting their trespasses against them... For our sake [God] made [Christ] to be sin who knew no sin, so that in him we might become the righteousness of God" (2 Corinthians 5:19, 21).

Paul's original rejection of Jesus as the accursed of God was based on his superficial reading of Deuteronomy 21:23 which pronounced "cursed...every one who...hanged on a tree". However Saul the persecutor was struck down near Damascus by the brightness of a light shining from God. The voice speaking from the light identified himself as "Jesus, whom you are persecuting" (Acts 9:5). Since for the Jew brightness or "glory" could only come from God, Paul knew in an instant that God was with Jesus and in Jesus. Paul's understanding of Jesus was turned upside down and inside out in that moment. Paul must have begun to understand from that time that Jesus did not die as a sinner, but *for* sinners, not as the accursed of God on his own account but on account of others, that God made him a sin offering for us (2 Corinthians 5:21).

Naturally Paul's understanding was very significantly shaped by the traditions of the Lord's Supper and the gospel-outline received from the "apostles before him" in the Jerusalem church (cf Galatians 1:17-19). These traditions in particular declared Jesus to be Messiah/Christ who had died *for* (Greek = *hyper*) his people (1 Corinthians 11:24-25; 15:3). Henceforth Paul will constantly teach and write "Christ died for us/you".

4 Baptized into Christ Jesus

If the twin pillars of the gospel of Christ were the death of the Messiah/Christ for sins and his resurrection from the dead, these two elements were also fundamental in the baptism of those who accepted the gospel. Those who were baptized were said to have been (somehow) incorporated into the death and resurrection of the Messiah/Christ: "...we have been united with [Christ] in a death like his, we shall...be united with [Christ] in a resurrection like his." (Romans 6:3-5)

Believers, therefore, "belong to [Christ]...who has been raised from the dead" (Romans 7:4). The crucified and risen Christ thus has a people who belong to him and who are spiritually joined to him now and who will be physically united with him at his coming.

The congregation into which the believer is baptized is actually called "Christ"; it is a messianic community. Paul asks the Corinthians: "Do you not know that your bodies are members of Christ?" (1 Corinthians 6:15; 12:12-13 cf 1:13). These members have heard and believed the Gospel of Christ, focusing as it does on Christ's death for sins and his resurrection, and they have been baptized into that Christ—they are united with him in his death and resurrection.

There are clear points of contact in Paul's presentation of the Christ and Jesus' teaching about the Son of Man:

a) The Son of Man has a people who are joined to him (the "saints of the most high"); so too, the Christ has a messianic community (the "body" of the Messiah) (Daniel 7:13–28; Mark 2:27; 1 Corintians 12: 12–13).

b) The Son of Man died in substitution for his people; so too, Christ dies for our sins (Mark 10:45; 1 Corinthians 15:3).

c) The Son of Man inaugurates the kingdom of God; so too, the Christ has a kingdom which he exercises on behalf of God (Matthew 25:31–34;1 Corinthians 15:27–28; Ephesians 5:5).

These points of contact are the more impressive because the terminology used is different. But the ideas are the same.

We are reminded once more of Jesus' call of the Twelve to be the embryo of the new people of God. They are the tiny seed which will grow into the great tree, the little flock which will be greatly enlarged, the rock onto which others will be built. Above all they and those who will be attached to them are the ones for whom he died, with whom he made covenant, and who would receive his kingdom. Paul restates this teaching in his references to Christ, his body and his kingdom.

SON OF GOD

The Letters of Paul clearly show that Jesus was also known as "the Son of God". Paul calls Jesus "the Son of God" four times, "the Son" twice and "his Son" eleven times. The second letter to the Corinthians indicates that Paul, Silvanus and Timothy proclaimed Jesus as "the Son of God" in Corinth in 50 (1:19). In the same year Paul wrote from Corinth to Thessalonica reminding the church that they had (recently) received a message which declared Jesus to be the heavenly "Son" of God ("his Son"—1 Thessalonians 1:10). We can say with confidence that Jesus was proclaimed to be and confessed to be the Son of God in 50 in both Thessalonica and Corinth.

It is highly unlikely that Paul only began to proclaim Jesus as Son of God during his missionary tour of the Greek archipelago. The letter to the Galatians, directed to churches which were established in the late forties was (in my opinion) written from Antioch c 49 before Paul set out on the tour that would take him to Thessalonica and Corinth. Paul wrote:

When the time had fully come,
God sent forth   his   Son
                                              born of a woman

                                              born under the law
to redeem those who were   under the law
so that we
may receive adoption as   sons.
And because you are   sons,
God sent forth the Spirit of his   Son
into our hearts crying *Abba*,
Father

(Galatians 4:4–6)

This statement, which may have been a church creed adapted by Paul for the Galatians, teaches that:

1 The new age has begun (*when the time had fully come*)

2 Jesus' pre-existence (the *Son* God *sent forth)*

3 The Son was fully human (*born of a woman*)

4 The Son had been brought up as a Jew (*born under the Law*)

5 The Son in his Spirit had called God *Abba*

6 Because the Spirit of the Son is now sent forth the Galatian and other Christians also call God *Abba*

The Son's historical relationship to God as *Abba* is the source of the Galatians' relationship with God as *Abba*. God's new age has been inaugurated by two sendings—the sending of his Son into the world and the sending of the Spirit of his Son into the hearts of believers.

Earlier than this, in c.34, not more than two years after the crucifixion, the Acts of the Apostles states that Saul upon his conversion immediately proclaimed Jesus as the Son of God in the synagogues of Damascus (9:20). While some may doubt the strict historicity of the Acts at this point it is noteworthy that this is the only occasion Jesus is referred to as "the Son of God" in the Acts of the Apostles. Moreover, Paul himself, in a reference to what happened near Damascus that can scarcely be doubted, specifically says that God revealed "his Son" to him at that very time (Galatians 1:16). We may be confident that, in fact, Paul proclaimed Jesus as Son of God as early as c.34. When Paul returned to his native Cilicia in c.36 he proclaimed "the faith he had once tried to destroy", that is the faith that Jesus was the Son of God (Galatians 1:23; cf 1:16). It must be regarded as a secure fact of history that Paul proclaimed Jesus to be the Son of God from c.36.

Another of the passages in which "Son of God" occurs also appears to have been a creed from earlier times, which Paul incorporates in his Letter to the Romans:

...the gospel of God...
concerning   his Son
                who was descended from David
                according to the flesh
and designated Son of God in power according to the
                Spirit...by his resurrection from the
                dead...

(Romans 1:3-4)

This passage teaches that:

1 The historical Jesus was God's [pre-existent?] Son, and,
2 The historical Jesus was, by physical descent, also the son of David—the Messiah.
3 By his resurrection from the dead, as witnessed by the coming of the Holy Spirit, this Son of God/son of David is now re-designated "Son of God in power".

Those who declared Jesus to be the "Son of God in power" did so on the basis of their experience both of his resurrection (the first Easter) and of the coming of the Holy Spirit (the day of Pentecost).

This important passage implies *continuity, exaltation and recognition*—the *continuity* beyond death of this Son of God/son of David, the *exaltation* of this person through resurrection at the first Easter and the *recognition* from the time of the first Pentecost that he is to be understood to be the "Son of God in power".

It is of utmost significance that Paul continues immediately in Romans 1: "Jesus Christ, our Lord".

The historical Jesus who was both Son of God and son of David who is now by his resurrection and the coming of the Holy Spirit attested to be Son of God in power *is* "Jesus Christ our Lord".

THE LORD

"Lord" (Greek: *kyrios*) is the most common title for Jesus in the letters of Paul. It is widely used in the undisputed earliest of Paul's letters—first and second Thessalonians and first and second Corinthians.

Kyrios is the word used for Yahweh, Israel's God, in the Greek translation of the Old Testament (called the Septuagint or LXX). It is highly significant that *kyrios* is applied to Jesus as the preferred way of referring to him. Many scholars, however, have challenged this connection between Jesus and Yahweh, pointing out (correctly) that *kyrios*, especially when used in the vocative ("O Lord") means no more than "sir" as a respectful form of address.

However, it is beyond doubt that Paul often uses *kyrios* to identify Jesus (in some way) with Yahweh. This may be seen in the way Paul applies to Jesus a number of texts from the Greek Old Testament which refer to the *Kyrios* = Yahweh, God of Israel.

Psalm 46:5 (LXX):
God is gone up with a shout, the *Kyrios* with the sound of the trumpet

1 Thessalonians 4:16:
The *Kyrios* (Jesus)...will descend with the sound of the trumpet

Joel 2:32 (LXX):
Whosoever will call on the name of the *Kyrios* will be saved

Romans 10:9–13:
For, every one who calls upon the name of the *Kyrios* will be saved.

Isaiah 45:22-24 (LXX):
I am God...there is
none other...to me every
knee shall bend, and
every tongue shall swear
by God

Philippians 2:10-11:
At the name of Jesus
every knee should
bow...and every tongue
confess that Jesus Christ
is *kyrios*...

Comparison between these texts leaves no doubt that Jesus the *kyrios* was regarded in terms identical to or at least similar to Yahweh the *kyrios*, the God of Israel.

On three occasions Paul uses the phrase "Jesus [Christ] is *kyrios*". On each occasion these words are "confessed" or "said" (Romans 10:9; 1 Corinthians 12:3; Philippians 2:11). Since 1 Corinthians 12:3,12-13 is clearly a baptismal setting the words "Jesus is *kyrios*" , wherever they occur in Paul's letters, appear to be a new convert's public acknowledgement of the Lordship of Jesus made to a congregation prior to baptism (cf 1 Peter 3:15,21-22).

Kyrios is Paul's most characteristic way of referring to Jesus; the word occurs 222 times in his letters. When Paul speaks of Jesus' return he invariably speaks of him as the *kyrios* (e.g. 1 Thessalonians 4:16-17). Yet he will speak of the earthly Jesus under the same title e.g. the brothers of the Lord, the cup of the Lord, the table of the Lord (1 Corinthians 9:5; 10:21).

Paul writes of the *kyrios* with great reverence: "To this end Christ died and lived again, that he might be *Lord* both of the dead and the living" (Romans 14:9).

The commands of this risen Lord bind believers (e.g. 1 Corinthians 7:10). He is the Coming One (e.g. 1 Thessalonians 4:6), the Judge (e.g. 1 Corinthians 4:4), the One before whom every knee shall bow and every tongue confess his Lordship (Philippians 2:11)

But when did Jesus begin to be thought of by this exalted title? Was it originated by Paul?

It is probable that Philippians 2:5-11, quoted above, originally existed as a hymn which had been in use in the churches for some time before Paul wrote to the Philippians. Again, the use of the word *kyrios* is so pervasive in Paul's writings that it appears to have been in use for a considerable period of time before the first of his known letters was written in 50 or earlier.

In writing to the Corinthians in the middle fifties Paul uses the word for "Lord" in two languages—the Greek *kyrios* and the Aramaic *mara*: "If anyone does not love the *kyrios*, let him be anathema. *Marana tha* [= Our Lord, come]" (1 Corinthians 16:22).

The Aramaic *Mara* = Lord in all probability goes back to the original Aramaic-speaking disciples' prayer to their Lord: *tha* = come [back]. This invocation is reproduced in Greek at the end of the Book of Revelation, "Amen, come Lord Jesus" (22:19). The prayer to the Lord expressed initially in Aramaic came to be expressed also in Greek.

As with references in Paul to "Christ" and "Son of God" we find that Jesus as *kyrios* precedes the writing of Paul's letters by many years and can be traced back towards the time of Jesus. But this raises an important question.

How do we explain these titles of exaltation?

Traditional or "received" material in the letters of Paul, which are themselves no later than twenty years after Jesus, establish that immediately after his time Jesus was regarded in exalted ways—as the Christ, the Son of God and the Lord. How can this be explained?

Reduced to essentials, there are two basic possibilities to explain the application of these exalted titles to Jesus. One is that the Christians made more of Jesus than he really was. On this theory, Jesus was only a rabbi or prophet who lived and died, but who, after his death came to have these titles applied to him. Those who hold this view suggest that "Son of God" and "Lord" were religious titles current in the Greek world which were then conferred on Jesus.

This view, which which was popularized last century by William Bousset and this century by his pupil Rudolph Bultmann, has been more recently investigated and rejected by Martin Hengel in his monograph, *The Son of God*. Hengel shows that these titles were not borrowed by the early Christians from the Greek world. It may be agreed, however, that the religious environment of the Gentile mission in which there was some mention of "sons of God" and "lords" contributed to the prominence given to the proclamation that Jesus was, indeed, "*the* Son of God" and "*the* Lord".

In any case this explanation begs the question why anyone, least of all Jewish followers, would want to confer such exalted titles on a failed Jewish prophet or rabbi who had recently died in such shameful circumstances. We know from Josephus of Jewish revolutionary rabbis and prophets of those times who died violent deaths. None of them were survived by the movements they had established. Nor were they described by the vocabulary of exaltation which was so quickly applied to Jesus. Indeed in most cases their teachings were not remembered, beyond one or two concepts.

The other expanation, which is adopted here, is that exalted titles were applied to Jesus because he was in fact exalted—by his resurrection from the dead—and that Jesus came to be recognised and proclaimed as having the identity of which he was conscious.

It was pointed out in the previous chapter that the pre-Easter Jesus was conscious of being what he claimed to be the "Son of Man". He also had a sense of filial relationship with God, a commitment to fulfil the role of the Servant and an awareness that he was the Son of David.

With some exceptions and modifications the post-Easter Jesus is proclaimed in these same terms.

One exception is Jesus' preferred self-designation "Son of Man", a semitic title which does not appear in Paul's letters. Because it was a term which would have been meaningless to Gentiles, Paul did not use it of Jesus either in evangelism or worship. It is a tribute to their writers' faithfulness to history and to the historic Jesus that in the Gospels, written sometime after Paul's letters, "the Son of Man" is repeatedly on Jesus' lips, despite the fact that by the time the Gospels were written Jesus was not referred to in that way.

An example of the way Jesus' self-designation was modified for the sake of Gentiles was that of "Messiah". Paul translated "Messiah" into the Greek *Christos*. Moreover, *Christos* usually appears in Paul as Jesus' surname. (Nonetheless, as we have seen, *the* Christos does survive to some extent in Paul's letters as a title of Jesus.)

The best explanation for the survival in history of Jesus' consciousness that he was "Messiah" and "Son of God" is that he rose from the dead, as the writers of the New Testament unanimously agree that he did. The religious environment did not create titles of exaltation for Jesus; these emerged from Jesus' consciousness of his identity and from his exaltation. The Hellenistic religious environment of Paul's Gentile mission does explain the prominence he gave to "Son of God" and "Lord", on one hand, and the neglect of "Son of Man" and the modification of "Messiah", on the other.

A gap of only three or four years existed between Jesus and his original followers' first contact with the newly converted Paul. Following are three concepts which originated with Jesus and were transmitted by the earliest community of believers to Paul.

1 *Abba*, the Aramaic for one's father used in a close and intimate sense, as the attitude to God of the "sons" of God (Galatians 4:6; Romans 8:14–15) exactly coincides with the attitude to God of the one who called himself "the Son" of God (Mark 12:6; 13:32; 14:36).

How did this word come to be used in the Greek-speaking churches in the forties and fifties unless it had been first treasured by the Aramaic-speaking believers? And why would it have been remembered by Aramaic-speaking believers unless these first disciples had learned it from Jesus? And would it have been remembered and transmitted if Jesus had died and not been raised?

2 The standard preposition used with the death of Christ by Paul and other New Testament writers is "for" (Greek: *hyper*). A good example is in the gospel tradition which Paul "received" and "delivered" to the churches that: "Christ died *for* our sins" (1 Corinthians 15:3). What is the origin of this *hyper*? It is not the preposition used of the Suffering Servant in Isaiah 53.5 who suffers "for [*dia*] our sins" (LXX). The prepositions have different nuances. *Dia* means only that the people's sins caused the death of the servant; *hyper* means that Christ's death was in substitution for his people's sins. In fact, the *hyper* probably comes from Jesus himself, as the traditions about the Last Supper suggest:

1 Corinthians 15:24:
"This is my body which is for [*hyper*] you"

Luke 22:19-20:
"This is my body which is given for [*hyper*] you... This cup is poured out for [*hyper*] you"

The New Testament contains many echoes of Isaiah 53 which, as we have noted, does not use *hyper* (but *dia).* The use of *hyper* appears to owe its origin to Jesus and the references he made to his death at the Last Supper, references which were remembered and treasured by his earliest community of disciples and passed on to Paul and others and through them to the Gentile churches.

3 Paul's favourite title for Jesus is *kyrios,* a Greek mode of reference translating the *Mara* which appears to have been used by earliest Aramaic-speaking disciples (1 Corinthians 16:22). Paul also speaks of the exalted Jesus as at "the right hand of God" (Romans 8:34).

Where do these ideas—"*Mara/kyrios*" and "at the right hand of God"—originate? The Gospels relate that Jesus used these categories in his question to the scribes: how was it possible for the Messiah to be the descendant of David? According to Jesus, David's words in Psalm 110 refers to the Messiah: "The *kyrios* [= Yahweh] said to my *kyrios* [= the Messiah] 'sit at my right hand...'"

Here is the Messiah commanded to sit at Yahweh's right hand. Jesus' question, recorded in Mark 12:37, was: since David's Lord was the Messiah at the time of writing the Psalm how is it possible for the Messiah also to be the son or descendant of David?

Jesus alone knew the answer to this riddle. He himself was the answer; *he* was the son of David who would very soon be David's Lord, the Messiah, seated at God's right hand.

This riddle was understood by the disciples of Jesus who witnessed his resurrection and who, in the light of that resurrection proclaimed Jesus to be indeed both "Lord" and "Christ" (son of David) in terms of Psalm 110:1 (Acts 2:36).

According to the Gospel of Mark Jesus had referred to himself before this incident as "Lord" (5:19; 11:3). This is striking since Jesus often referred to the God of Israel as "Lord" (11:9; 12:9; 12:29–30). In Psalm 110, which Jesus quoted in his question to the scribes, "Lord" is understood by Jesus as referring both to Yahweh and to the Messiah.

Mark's careful writing should be noted at this point. Jesus is never addressed by the disciples as "Lord"; Jesus alone speaks of himself using that word. The disciples address Jesus in Aramaic, "rabbi", or its Greek equivalent, "teacher". The disciples also refer to him as "the teacher". In other words, although Jesus himself told his disciples that he was "Lord" and this became the origin of the title which would predominate in the New Testament, the Gospel of Mark does not import that title back into the gospel narrative and place it on the lips of the disciples.

Thus the explanation which best fits the fact of exalted titles being applied to Jesus is that he was indeed exalted by his resurrection from the dead. Jesus, "the Son of Man" was conscious that he was "Messiah", "Son of God", "Lord" and "Servant" of God. What happened to him—his death and resurrection—confirmed to those who had been with him that his claims and consciousness were well founded. In particular, had he not been raised from the dead the identity of which he was conscious and which can be detected within the Gospels would have been ridiculous and absurd, and indeed would have been quickly and gladly forgotten.

The chain of revelation from Jesus through the Twelve to Paul and through him to the churches may be expressed as follows:

JESUS as

Son of Man	→ The Twelve → Jerusalem church → Paul?
Son of God	→ The Twelve → Jerusalem church → Paul → churches
Abba	→ The Twelve → Jerusalem church → Paul → churches
Lord	→ The Twelve → Jerusalem church → Paul → churches
hyper sins	→ The Twelve → Jerusalem church → Paul → churches
the Christ/Messiah	→ The Twelve → Jerusalem church → Paul → churches

Who are you, Lord?

Near Damascus, Saul, arch-persecutor of Christians, was thrown to the ground by a brilliant light from which a voice addressed him. Paul replied, "Who are you Lord?" (Acts 9:5). The voice identified himself. "I am Jesus...".

This is important. It may be thought that this exalted figure who was called Christ, Son of God and the Lord was devoid of personality, a divine sovereign who lacked any human qualities. That, certainly, is the way he appears in religious art in the middle ages. One has only to think of the impassive figure who is portrayed in stained glass or on Byzantine icons.

What we find in the letters of the New Testament, however, is that many of the human aspects of the personality of the historical Jesus are to found in their references to the exalted Lord. There is no discontinuity between the historic figure of Jesus and the Jesus who is the object of the worship of the early Christians.

These human characteristics of the historic Jesus appear when Paul is encouraging the churches to behave in particular ways.

The Roman Christians, who were divided into Jewish and Gentile groups which met separately, are exhorted to: "Welcome one another...as Christ has welcomed you" (Romans 15:7). This calls to mind Christ's gracious invitation "Come to me" which he often made (e.g. Matthew 11:28).

The Philippians were behaving proudly in their relations with one another, and this was affecting their church's unity. Paul asks them to: "Do nothing from selfishness or conceit", to live in "humility" and to "look to the interests...of others". In other words, to live according to the "mind of Christ" (Philippians 2:3-5). This too is in line with Jesus' known character. He said: "I am gentle and lowly in heart" (Matthew 11:29).

The Corinthians were so preoccupied with themselves that they showed little sensitivity to the needs of outsiders, including their need for the salvation of God. Paul urges them to *seek* for the good of their neighbours, "that they may be saved". Again, Christ is given as an example: "Be imitators of me, as I am of Christ" (1 Corinthians 11.1). Paul's words echo the words of Jesus to the tax collector, Zacchaeus: "The Son of Man came to seek and to save the lost" (Luke 19.10).

The Corinthians also regarded Paul's ministry as weak and ineffectual. But they were judging the apostle by the aggressive standards of the day. Paul has to say to them: "I . . . entreat you, by the meekness and gentleness of Christ" (2 Corinthians 11:1). Once more we are reminded that Jesus was "gentle" and "lowly" (Matthew 11:29).

Paul is not alone in writing of the Exalted One in terms of his human characteristics. The writer to the Hebrews, for example, speaks of Jesus as "the great shepherd" and as a "high priest" who is able to "sympathize with our weaknesses" and to show "mercy" and "grace to help in time of need" (13:20; 4:15–16). As high priest Jesus is the source of our salvation because he became perfect in the obedience he showed to God during his life (5:7–9).

Peter also points to the example of the human Jesus in not threatening those who were killing him, but rather commending his way to God in faith (1 Peter 2:23). Here we think of Jesus at Golgotha when he prayed that God would forgive those who were executing him (Luke 23:34).

It is clear, therefore, that Paul and other writers of the post-Jesus period often reminded their readers of the example of the historic Jesus. Moreover, the historical Lord, who is now through death and resurrection the heavenly Lord, has taken his human personality intact with him into heaven. As Jesus was, so he is and will continue to be. He reacted to suffering with compassion and to injustice with anger. He displayed the full range of emotions, being both meek and majestic. But we relate to him now as if we were relating to him then, as recorded in the Gospels. The heavenly Lord whom we worship and serve is the historical Lord, exalted to the right hand of the Father.

How did Paul know about these human qualities of Jesus? The Gospels, it should be noted, were written after Paul. Therefore Paul must have heard about Jesus' character from those who were Christians before him. Ultimately a knowledge of these human qualities of Jesus as mentioned in the letters of Paul to the churches must have arisen from

Jesus' impact on the Twelve and through them to the apostle Paul. Paul's stay with Cephas in Jerusalem for fifteen days in c. 36 would have provided the opportunity for Paul to learn about the human character of the Lord whom he was now serving (Galatians 1:18).

Further Reading:

P.W. Barnett, *Is the New Testament History?*, (Sydney, Hodder & Stoughton, 1984/Ann Arbor, Servant, 1987)

W. Bousset, *Kyrios Christos*, (Nashville, Abingdon Press, 1970)

M. Hengel, *The Son of God*, (London, SCM, 1976)

——*Between Jesus and Paul*, (London, SCM, 1983)

A.M. Hunter, *Paul and his Predecessors*, (London, SCM, 1961)

J. Jeremias, *The Central Message of the New Testament*, (London, SCM, 1965)

12 THE EXALTED ONE IN THE LETTER TO THE HEBREWS

This anonymous writer specifically attributes his understanding about Jesus to those who had heard the Lord and who in turn had spoken to the writer and his readers. This letter is very Jewish in tone, yet we find no hint of the New Quest profile of Jesus. Rather we find a powerful affirmation that Jesus is the eternal Son of God who is now the true high priest of God's people.

Paul's letters have been a major source of evidence for the identity of Jesus. This is because they are so numerous, so close in time to Jesus and also because we can establish their precise dates of composition (for the most part) with such high confidence. These remarkable letters arguably provide the earliest external historical information for any notable person in antiquity.

Another very important source of information about Jesus is found in the so-called letter to the Hebrews. The significance of this letter is that, unlike Paul's letters, it was written to *Jewish* readers. Perhaps in this letter we will find echoes of Jesus as rabbi or prophet? Not only do we find no such echoes, we find, rather, statements of high exaltation about Jesus.

The writer of this "word of exhortation", as he calls it (13:22), nowhere identifies himself or his readers. Nonetheless there are a number of clues as to when the letter was written and for what purpose, matters which relate significantly to questions about Jesus.

When the letter declares "our brother Timothy has been released, with whom I shall see you if he comes soon" (13:23) we take it that the letter was written sometime after the conversion of Timothy in c. 48 (Acts 16:1). Many references in the letter suggest the temple was still in use at the time of writing (5:1-4; 8:13; 9:6; 10:1-3; 13:10-14). Since the war in which the temple was destroyed broke out in 66 we may take it that Hebrews must have been written prior to that time. This means the letter to the Hebrews was written sometime between c.48-c.65, that is within the general time frame of the writing of Paul's letters. The letter to the Hebrews, therefore, is a very early witness to Jesus, at earliest 15 years removed from him, at latest only about 30 years later than his historic ministry.

The author and his readers did not hear the message of salvation from the Lord himself but from his original hearers (2:3). Here is a very clear statement by a New Testament writer of his dependence on Jesus' original circle of hearers, and beyond them to Jesus himself. Their hearing of this message was accompanied by "signs and wonders and various miracles and by gifts of the Holy Spirit" (2:4). The period after the historic Jesus was marked by supernatural manifestations and it was in the context of these that the writer and his readers first heard the message about Jesus. Whether this refers to speech in other tongues on the day of Pentecost as described in Acts 2 or to the numerous miracles of the first two or three years of the Jerusalem community as set out in Acts 3-6 is not clear. But it seems likely that their conversion occurred somewhere within this earliest period.

That time, however, was also one of great suffering, with public abuse, the loss of property and the imprisonment of members (10:32-39; 6:10). Here the analogy of the two faces of Jesus should be noted. Clearly the persecutors of this group were strongly opposed to Jesus, though their precise perception of him cannot be deduced from the letter. Their impression of Jesus, whatever it was, led them to oppose the group to whom the author is writing. The writer and his readers, for their part, while seeing Jesus in terms of his historical profile, saw his filial face very clearly. Their understanding of Jesus in those terms was directly dependent upon the Twelve (2:3-4).

Though time has passed since the original persecution, some members are still in prison, possibly the same ones (13:3). At the time of writing there is renewed hostility towards the readers (12:3-4), with significant pressure applied to reject Jesus as the Son of God (6:6; 10:29). The author urges his readers to "hold fast the confession of our hope" and not to "shrink back" (10:23,39).

Who are these people? According to the letter they were Jews, "descendants of Abraham", (2:16 cf 1:1) who were living in or near Jerusalem (13:10-14). Since the letter is written in Greek we assume the readers were Greek-speaking Jews. The strong antipathy to the temple implied in the letter may mean that the writer and his readers shared views similar to Stephen and the Hellenist Jewish believers whom we encounter in Acts 6-7. Perhaps the writer/readers were in fact Hellenists who remained in Jerusalem, unlike Philip and others who were were "scattered" far and wide after the onslaught of Saul (Acts 8; 9:31; 11:19-20). Certainly we know of believers who were publicly punished and imprisoned at that time (Acts 26:10-11).

In recent times these believers have made little spiritual progress and now, when there is renewed suffering, they are in danger of relinquishing their commitment to Jesus and being absorbed back into Judaism (5:11-6:12; 10:19-39; 12:1-13; 13:7-17).

The writer's chief argument in encouraging his readers to remain believers is the greatness of Jesus. The letter is really a sustained, closely reasoned case from beginning to end for the superiority of Jesus—to angels, to the Levitical priesthood, to the sacrifices, to the covenant, to the temple, and to Mount Zion. Indeed, the sacrifices of the former covenant are now abolished by the death of Jesus (10:9). It is implied that those believers who are Levitical priests are to turn away from the altar of the temple (13:9-14).

Archaeological investigation made possible since the consolidation of the modern state of Israel after 1967 has revealed how substantial Jerusalem and its temple were in Jesus' day.

At the time this letter was written greater Jerusalem may have been a city of a quarter of a million permanent residents. Its great temple, built by Herod, stood on a massive marble platform equivalent in size to twelve soccer fields. Thousands of priests were involved in the service of that cultus. Hundreds of thousands of Jews streamed into Jerusalem for the great feasts, especially the feast of Passover. During the bitter war between Jews and Romans in Palestine 66–70, Jewish patriots defended their city and finally their temple with fanatical dedication. Tens of thousands of Jews died defending the name of Yahweh their God who, they were convinced, was manifested in the temple, the priesthood and the sacrifices.

The whole argument of the letter to the Hebrews is that *one* man is so much more more important than the temple that it is now irrelevant. But how could that be when thousands thought that their lives were less important than the temple, so that they were prepared to die for it? Which man could possibly outweigh the importance and significance of the temple of God standing on Mt Zion?

The answer lies in the exceptional and unique greatness of that man.

Space does not permit an extensive examination of this letter's assertions about Jesus which are arguably the most exalted of the New Testament.

Following is a selection of passages from Hebrews illustrating the remarkable exaltation of the person of Jesus, written less than three decades after Jesus when the temple and its sacrificial system was at the pinnacle of its greatness. In the first we encounter Jesus as the *Son of God*:

> In these last days [God] has spoken to us by a Son, whom he appointed heir of all things, through whom also he created the worlds. He reflects the glory of God and bears the very stamp of his nature, upholding the universe by his word of power. When he had made purification for sins, he sat down at the right hand of the majesty on high, having become as much superior to angels as the name he has obtained is more excellent than theirs... But of

the Son [God] says, "Thy throne, O God, is forever and ever" (1:2-4,8).

In the second, Jesus is also the great *high priest*:

Since then we have a great high priest who has passed through the heavens, Jesus, the Son of God, let us hold fast our confession (4:14).

In the third, the author presents Jesus also as the *priest-king Melchizedek*:

We have this as sure and steadfast anchor of the soul, a hope that enters into the inner shrine behind the curtain, where Jesus has gone as a forerunner on our behalf, having become a high priest forever after the order of Melchizedek... [Melchizedek] is, first, by translation of his name, king of righteousness, and then he is also king of Salem, that is, king of peace. He is without father or mother or genealogy, and has neither beginning of days nor end of life, but resembling the Son of God, he continues a priest forever (6:19-7.3).

In the fourth, Jesus is *the sacrifice* to end all sacrifices:

When Christ came into the world, he said, "Sacrifices and offerings thou hast not desired, but a body thou hast prepared for me; in burnt offerings and sin offerings thou hast taken no pleasure. Then I said, 'Lo I have come to do thy will, O God,' as it is written of me in the roll of the book"... [Jesus] abolishes the first [i.e. the sacrifices] in order to establish the second [i.e. to do God's will]. And by that will we have been sanctified through the offering of the body of Jesus Christ once and for all (10:5-10).

It might be thought that this Jesus is so exalted, so eternal a character as to lack identifiable humanity. But this is not the case. No part of the New Testament makes more of the humanity of Jesus than this letter.

Jesus was descended from the tribe of Judah (7:14), he spoke about salvation (2:3), he was subjected to temptation to which, however, he did not succumb (4:15), he endured great hostility against himself (12:3) and he remained faithful over God's house as his Son (3:6).

One passage, in particular, expresses Jesus' sufferings in a powerful way. These words probably refer to his death:

In the days of his flesh, Jesus offered up prayers and

supplications, with loud cries and tears, to him who was able to save him from death, and he was heard for his godly fear. Although he was a son, he learned obedience through what he suffered; (5:7–8).

Jesus' faithfulness to God in suffering and death is his qualification to be the "source of eternal salvation to all those who obey him" (5:9). As a persevering and righteous sufferer Jesus is the "pioneer" or exemplar-leader of God's people to their salvation (2:10; 12:1–2).

This letter is in effect, a tangible historical artefact. Its affirmations raise powerful questions about the historical Jesus—who was he? Somebody wrote it out of profound convictions about Jesus. Where did those convictions come from? The effect, the letter, lies open before us. The question is what caused the effect?

Logic demands that somebody very great and remarkable impacted on the people of his generation for such a letter to have been written, somebody as great and remarkable as the Gospels declare Jesus to have been. As with the writings of Paul this book has a strong view of Jesus as the Son (of God). Our argument is that Jesus' filial consciousness was the source of the understanding of the Twelve who in turn transmitted this understanding to Paul and the anonymous author, whose writings are independent of each other.

What, then, of those recent Jesuses as suggested by Vermes and Sanders? Could a rabbi or prophet have inspired this anonymous Jewish author to say that the temple was less important, indeed now redundant? Would this writer have called for a life or death commitment to such a Jesus, now deceased for some years?

Common sense demands that these unremarkable figures could not have lain behind the exalted and eternal Jesus we meet in this letter. Only the unforgettable, divine figure, as raised from the dead, could have made the impact on his generation which is presupposed in this letter.

Further reading:
J. Jeremias, *Jerusalem in the Time of Jesus*, (London, SCM, 1969)

B. Mazar, "Excavations near Temple Mount reveals splendours of Herodian Jerusalem", *Biblical Archaeological Review*, (1980) vi/4, pp.44–59

H. Shanks, "Excavating in the Shadow of the Temple Mount", *Biblical Archaeological Review*, (1986) xii/6, pp.20-49

13 IMAGES OF DEITY

The letters of the New Testament contain a stunning array of deity images as applied to Jesus. How are we to account for these except through the impact Jesus made on the Twelve?

As we read the New Testament, we are conscious that the writers are struggling to put into words their convictions about Jesus. It is plain that they thought of him as deity, though not so as to replace or displace the God who had revealed himself under the old covenant. The next centuries would witness the intellectual struggle to understand how the Lord Jesus and the Holy Spirit related to God and how Jesus could be both man and God. The New Testament does not provide systematic answers to those questions. But it does provide the raw material on which the creeds of the church would be based.

A brief survey of the New Testament for reference to the deity of Jesus now follows. This survey is neither comprehensive nor exhaustive, but rather illustrative in character. No reference is made to the Gospels or the Acts of the Apostles; our focus is on the letters of the New Testament.

The *apostle Paul* writes of Jesus as the "Lord of Glory" (1 Corinthians 2:8). He can speak interchangeably of the "glory of Christ" and the "glory of God" (2 Corinthians 4:6). In biblical thought glory belongs to God alone: "I am Yahweh and I shall not give my glory to another" (Isaiah 42:8).

Paul also writes of Jesus as the judge, before whose
judgement seat all must appear (2 Corinthians 5:10; cf 2
Timothy 4:1). In the Old Testament Yahweh is the judge of
all the earth and of the nations (Genesis 18:25; Joel 3:12).
In one passage Jesus is called "God" by Paul:

To them [i.e. the Jewish people] belong the patriarchs,
and of their race, according to the flesh, is the Christ,
who is God over all blessed forever. (Romans 9:5)

Although this passage is subject to different translations (see
e.g. RSV), the rendering given above is, in the opinion of
many, correct.

The *writer to the Hebrews* specifically addresses Jesus as
God: "Thy throne, O God, is for ever and ever", he wrote
(1:8). According to this writer he is "Our Lord Jesus, the
great shepherd of the sheep" (13:20). Shepherd is an Old
Testament image for God (Psalm 23:1; Ezekiel 34:15).

The *letter of James* is thought to represent the most extreme
form of Judaic Christianity in the New Testament. There
is no reference to the atoning death of Jesus; the emphasis
is on ethical teaching, in which many echoes of Jesus'
teaching may be heard. Nonetheless, James takes the deity
of Jesus for granted. He refers on a number of occasions
to the God of Israel as "Lord" (3:9; 4:8, 10:5-4,10) yet he
also calls Jesus "Lord", indeed the "Lord of glory" (1:1; 2:1;
5:7,8,11).

The *first letter of Peter* calls on its readers "in your hearts
reverence Christ as Lord" (3:15). Peter here substitutes *Christ*
for "the Lord of hosts...*he* shall be your fear" in Isaiah
8:13. Peter's reference to Christ as a "stone" for the people
of God (2:4-8) is meant to evoke images of Yahweh as Israel's
"rock" (cf Genesis 49:24; Psalm 18:2; 95:1; Isaiah 28:16).
Jesus' designation as "chief shepherd" of the "brotherhood
which is throughout the whole world" is also intended to
remind us of Yahweh, shepherd of Israel (5:4,9; cf Psalm 80:1)

The *second letter of Peter* specifically refers to Jesus as "our
God and saviour Jesus Christ" and "our Lord and saviour
Jesus Christ" (1:1,11). In the Old Testament Yahweh is often

spoken of as saviour, for example, "I am Yahweh, thy God, the holy one of Israel, thy saviour" (Isaiah 43:3).

In his *first letter, John* leaves us in no doubt as to his attitude to Jesus:

> We know that the Son of God has come and has given us understanding, to know him who is true; and we are in him who is true, in his Son Jesus Christ. This is the true God and eternal life.   (5.20)

It is significant that truth was one of the attributes of the God of Israel (see e.g. Psalm 25:10; 40:10). Here, as often in the New Testament, truth is applied to Jesus.

In the *Book of Revelation* the "one like a Son of man" has "hair...white like wool" (1:13-14). But this is the appearance of the Ancient of Days, God (Daniel 7:9). The Lamb and God occupy the *one* throne (22:3), signifying their essential oneness. The Lord God Almighty states "I am the Alpha and Omega" (1:8); but so too does Jesus (22:13). Significantly, Jesus adds the words "[I am] the first and the last" (also: 1:17; 2:8; 22:13). But in the prophet Isaiah Yahweh declares himself to be "first and last" (41:4; 44:6; 48:12). The Lamb is portrayed as a redeemer: "Thou wast slain and didst ransom men for God" (5:9). Once again we note a parallel with the God of Israel: he is a redeemer (Psalm 130:7; Hosea 13:14). Clearly we are meant to understand Jesus the Lamb in terms of Yahweh.

Jesus is but one of many leaders who arose at that time in Jewish Palestine. But he alone was regarded as an object of divine worship; no rabbi or prophet was so venerated. John the Baptist had some following after his death, but it could not be thought of as a movement (Mark 2:18; Acts 19:1-8). Jesus alone was survived by the movement he established, a movement which vigorously promoted allegiance to him as the risen Lord, a movement which in time produced for its members as well as outsiders the body of literature we call the New Testament. Enough has been written to illustrate that Paul, the writer to the Hebrews, James, Peter (in both his letters) and John (in both 1 John and the Revelation) each ascribe deity to Jesus. There is great variety in the manner of referring to Jesus, yet we are left in no doubt about his uniqueness and deity.

What is the origin of these images of Jesus which we find within the New Testament? Historically speaking the essential idea that Jesus is the Son of God must have come through the Twelve, though the various authors express that idea in their own ways (largely influenced by imagery associated with Yahweh in the Old Testament).

But the Twelve did not invent the notion that Jesus was the Son of God. It was Jesus who revealed to the Twelve his filial relationship to God. To the Galileans of the period who observed him, however, Jesus remained a rabbi, a prophet of the kingdom of God—an oblique character who taught in mystifying parables and cast out demons. Many New Quest scholars, while displaying enviable historical expertise remain at arm's length from Jesus; he is for them what he was for those Galileans—a rabbi or prophet.

14 JESUS: THE OPTIONS

To those who saw, and still see, only one face, Jesus remains an enigma, for whom novel interpretations continue to be offered. But those who stand in the shoes of the Twelve, as expressed in the New Testament, also see the filial face of Jesus. That Jesus in fact had that face is the most logical explanation for the attitude of the New Testament towards him.

Who, then, was he, this Jesus?

The twenty-seven books which make up that small library known as the New Testament, came from the pens of nine different authors:

Paul	13 letters
Author of Hebrews	1 letter
James	1 letter
Peter	2 letters
Jude	1 letter
John	1 gospel; 3 letters; 1 apocalypse
Mark	1 gospel
Matthew	1 gospel
Luke	1 gospel; 1 acts

These works were written between c. 50–95. For the most part the authors write independently of each other. Matthew and Luke know Mark. John, author of the Revelation, alludes to the Gospels of Matthew and John and the letters of Paul. Apart from these, the writers betray no dependence on others.

What is truly remarkable is that, in each of these writings, Jesus is the focal point. No part of the New Testament would have been written except for Jesus. The rest of the New Testament literature, therefore, is exactly the same as the Jesus-movement as reflected in the letters of Paul—Jesus is its sole *raison d'être*, its preoccupation.

This literature is rich in its devotion to Jesus. As many as forty-two different names and titles of Jesus from the New Testament are listed by Vincent Taylor in his book *The Names of Jesus*. Taylor points to the power and applicability of these early names and titles of Jesus, contrasting them with the dismal efforts of hymn-writers and others in later centuries.

In the earliest preaching of Peter, as recorded in the Acts of the Apostles, Jesus is proclaimed as Christ, Lord, the Prophet, God's Servant, the Holy One, the Righteous One, the Pioneer, Saviour and Rock.

In the writings of Paul, in addition to the titles of exaltation, which we have already considered, Jesus is referred to as the Image of God, the Firstborn, the Wisdom of God, the Saviour, the Mediator, our Peace and the Last Adam.

According to the writer of the letter to the Hebrews Jesus is the Son of God, our great High Priest, the pioneer of faith and the great Shepherd of the sheep.

The writings of John contain a dazzling array of titles. In the Gospel of John Jesus is presented as the King of Israel, the Son of man, the only begotten Son, the bread of life, the light of the world, the door of the sheep, the good shepherd, the vine, the resurrection, the way and the truth and the life. In his letters, John writes of Jesus as the Paraclete and the Expiation. In the Revelation, Jesus is Lion of the Tribe of Judah, the Lamb that was slain, the bright and morning star, the Alpha and Omega, the first and the last, the Word of God, to mention just some of his titles.

The Gospels portray those who met Jesus acknowledging him in what can only be called extraordinary terms. In Mark, the Roman centurion declares Jesus as crucified to be "truly the Son of God". In Matthew, Peter confesses Jesus to be "the Christ, the Son of the Living God". In John, Thomas speaks to Jesus as "my Lord and my God".

This literature, which is written close on time to Jesus,

and by so many independent authors, portrays Jesus in exalted and adoring terms. Truly he is a gigantic and divine figure. Though a Jew he bursts out of the racial and religious confines of Judaism. He is Lord of all men and women everywhere—Jews and Gentiles.

How stark the contrast, therefore, between Jesus as presented in the New Testament and the figure reconstructed in the writings of many New Quest scholars. Their message is clear. Jesus is a rabbi or a prophet; he cannot be a deity figure.

As we have argued, however, this perception of Jesus corresponds with the perception of him many Jews had at that time. His message of the kingdom of God did resemble that of John the Baptist; like rabbis of the day he did teach in the synagogue and have disciples.

Thus there were two perceptions of Jesus—one to the people at large; the other to the Twelve. The former perception of Jesus is characterised by uncertainty. His precise role is disputed—is he a rabbi or a prophet? His morality is ambiguous—is he an admirable example of piety and courage or is he a charlatan? His profile is enigmatic, mystifying—how is it that a great movement arose because of him? This profile of Jesus was and remains deeply mysterious, capable of seemingly endless new interpretations, of which New Quest scholars form only a part. Thus new books and films periodically appear, stimulated by this fascinating but inexplicable person.

As part of the Jewish people at the time the Twelve doubtless saw him as prophet and or rabbi who spoke about the kingdom of God. Yet to them he revealed the face which was hidden from "those on the outside" (Mark 4:11). They came to understand that the kingdom of God was actualized by the Son of Man, that the Son of Man was also the Son of God (in the filial, not merely the popular messianic sense) and the servant of the Lord. Insofar as they recognised him to be the Christ, it was in terms radically redefined by him.

The difference between the Jesus of these scholars and the Jesus as presented in the New Testament could not be greater. A monumental error of judgement has therefore been made about Jesus—either by the writers of the New

Testament or by those recent writers who have depicted him in such minimal terms.

The challenge for us is: whose perception of Jesus do we share—that of the Jewish people of the time, currently echoed by New Quest scholars, who saw but one face of Jesus and who remains a riddle? Or do we share the perception of the Twelve as expressed in the New Testament?

In favour of the latter view it is noted that the New Testament writers were very close in time and place to Jesus. As Jews, (with the exception of Luke—Colossians 4:14,11), they would have found it impossible to regard a man as somehow on a par with their God, Yahweh, unless in fact he was. To regard Jesus in divine terms, as they did, necessitated overcoming massive theological and cultural presuppositions. For Jews to accept that God would save the Gentiles—with whom war was imminent—on the same terms as Israel, demanded a significant change of heart and mind.

Their love and commitment to Jesus cost them dearly, including in some cases their own lives. Their high view of Jesus brought them no benefit, only conflict and pain.

Why would the New Testament writers, and the Twelve on whom they depend, constantly declare Jesus to be the Son of God, the Christ and the Lord, unless in fact, he was?

Perhaps the error of judgement lies with the scholars who downgrade Jesus. Despite the great increase in their knowledge of the life and times of first century Palestine, and of sophisticated linguistic and exegetical techniques, it is possible that their insistence on fitting Jesus into the framework of the Judaism of the period has resulted in any evidence from outside that framework being disregarded.

The challenge is there for all of us to ask: who, after all, has Jesus right? Who was he? Who has made the gigantic mistake, the writers of the New Testament who say he was an exalted figure or those scholars who say that he was not— he was only a rabbi or a prophet? If the New Testament writers have it wrong, they have made what is arguably the biggest error of judgement in history—an error which has misled millions of people over nearly two thousand years.

If, however, the New Testament writers are right about Jesus, as we have argued throughout, then we must turn from those scholars who reduce Jesus to the size of ordinary men of his day. Rather, we must do as the nine writers of the New Testament do—bow down before Jesus as master and Lord, placing our lives and our destinies, including our eternal destinies, in his hands.

Further reading:
V. Taylor, *The Names of Jesus*, (London, Macmillan, 1953)